"This book is a very good read. I have to admit that until now I always took thinking for granted. I can almost hear the author say "that is pretty reptilian of you." Then I read this book and the whole thinking process became clear to me. In a strange way, there was a certain loss of innocence as the forces that drive the thought process were presented by the author. This book did not provide me with the ability to think, but instead with the ability to think about why I think a certain way. Confused? Pick this book up and read it, it will all become clear to you too."

—Augusto L. Vidaurreta, author of *New York Times* bestseller
Business Is a Contact Sport

"Lauren Powers has tackled a tough but enormously important topic—the power of our unconscious fears and negative assumptions to lead us astray. Loaded with fascinating stories and written with grace and flair, this is a book worth reading."

—Judith Sherven and James Sniechowski,
Authors of *Be Loved for Who You Really Are* and
The Smart Couple's Guide to the Wedding of Your Dreams

" *The Trouble with Thinking* will have you laughing your way to sanity. Powers is brilliantly clear as she outlines the problems our thinking creates. Her stories, research, and comic relief provide more than a few aha moments. Your troubles with thinking will soon be over."

—Melanie Dewberry-Jones, Spiritual Coach and
author of *What was God Thinking?*

The Trouble with Thinking

The Trouble with Thinking

✦

The Dangerous Trip from In the Head to Out the Mouth

Lauren Powers

iUniverse, Inc.
New York Lincoln Shanghai

The Trouble with Thinking
The Dangerous Trip from In the Head to Out the Mouth

iUniverse books may be ordered through booksellers or by contacting:

iUniverse
2021 Pine Lake Road, Suite 100
Lincoln, NE 68512
www.iuniverse.com
1-800-Authors (1-800-288-4677)

ISBN-13: 978-0-595-39396-1 (pbk)
ISBN-13: 978-0-595-83794-6 (ebk)
ISBN-10: 0-595-39396-9 (pbk)
ISBN-10: 0-595-83794-8 (ebk)

Printed in the United States of America

For Eric Vik, the fairest of them all

Contents

Acknowledgements

Writing is often solitary (and crazy making). But I felt so strongly supported while I worked on this book. I'm beaming gratitude for the following:

For the ideas of Chris Argyris, the James Bryant Conant Professor of Education and Organizational Behavior at Harvard Business School. Argyris, creator of the Ladder of Inference, is a pioneer in identifying how and why we defend ourselves from learning. Thanks to Motorola's dedication to employee development, I was encouraged to participate in workshops inspired by Argyris' teaching. I offer my deep appreciation to Action Design Associates, Collaborative Action Technologies, and Innovation Associates.

For The Coaches Training Institute. Founded by Laura Whitworth, Henry Kimsey-House and Karen Kimsey-House who are responsible for my learning how to talk *with* people, not *at* them. My years engaging with CTI and with coaches the world over are precious and irreplaceable.

For my friends and family who let me tell stories about them. Lansing Bicknell, Logynn Ferrall, Jeff Jacobson, Kathryn Leal-Powers, Michael McCown, Bill Powers, Joan Powers, Maura Powers, William Powers, Rick Tamlyn, Eric Vik, and Rosemary Vik. (The names and identifying details of everyone else in this book have been changed.)

For the graciousness of people who know what they're doing toward those of us who don't. Jay Acton, Jane Von Mehren, Angela Rinaldi, Judith Sherven & Jim Sniechowski, and Augusto L. Vidaurreta.

For my dogged comrades in writing (and re-writing and re-writing). Molly McCombs, Randi Voss, Cindy Yarbrough. Also, Christine McHugh, Jill Nagle, Michelle Stanush.

For my buds who've cheered me on with laughs, wisdom, and cattle prods. Lansing Bicknell, Leslie Clark, Melanie Dewberry-Jones, Sharna D. Fey, Jeff Jacobson, Jill Schropp, Judy Seropan.

For my parents who aren't sure what it is that I do but are proud nonetheless. Joan R. & William E. Powers.

Introduction

o o o o o o o o o o o o o o o o o o o o o o o o o o o o o o o o

The legendary baseball player Yogi Berra ordered a pizza for dinner.
When he was asked whether he wanted it cut into four or eight pieces,
he replied, "Better make it four. I don't think I could eat eight."

We're constantly forming opinions and making decisions—from how many pieces of pizza we want to why we'll never shop at that store again to who the love of our life truly is. But our brains are rarely engaged in our decision-making. Instead we run on autopilot, making up habitual negative stories about our lives and the people in them. Surprisingly, we rarely doubt these interpretations. We're unaware of how our emotions, our judgments, our upbringing, even our biochemistries effect us more than we would like. The brain, left to its own devices, can be a dangerous power tool.

Our faulty perceptions and memories, our off-base conclusions, and our dogged belief that we're right about everything inevitably lead to all manner of unhappiness—hurt feelings, antagonistic feuds, and serious mistakes. Sadly, our relationships, careers, and hopes fall victim to these misguided thoughts without our even noticing. The way to change this unconscious pattern is to pull back the curtain, a la *The Wizard of Oz*, and observe who is actually running the show.

I call this automatic process that determines so much of our lives, Rat Brain. The first step of Rat Brain Loop begins the moment we select, out of all that's happening in the world, what to pay attention to. We then process that information using a completely personal, idiosyncratic dictionary. Third, we label other people (or ourselves) in a disapproving way. In the fourth step, we act on our thoughts. These actions, which are based on inaccurate interpretations, usually make things worse. This, in a nutshell, is how we typically navigate through the world—painful, isn't it? Especially because each part of the Rat Brain Loop is biased, incomplete, and unreliable. We only notice what we want to notice, our memories are notoriously creative, and of course, our feelings can profoundly skew our thinking.

The good news is that these flaws are actually leverage points for change, for different thoughts, for new actions, and for more satisfying outcomes. We can be generous, discerning, and compassionately intelligent, when we use the whole of ourselves in our thinking. Enormous shifts are possible once we understand Rat Brain. We can make choices about how we interpret information, how we interact with people, and how to own our thinking instead of letting it own us. And frankly, life outside the Rat Brain Loop is not only wiser and deeper—but funnier.

1

The Benefit of Doubt: Knowing

o o o o o o o o o o o o o o o o o o o o o o o o o o o o o o o

At a New York party, the violinist Isaac Stern was introduced to Muhammad Ali, the heavy-weight boxing champion of the world.

"You might say we're in the same business," remarked Stern. "We both earn a living with our hands."

"You must be pretty good," said Ali. "There isn't a mark on you."

Ali's joke is a perfect example of how we create meaning; we invent stories, explanations, and rationales from a tidbit of information and an entirely personal perspective. Unfortunately, like Ali, we can be way off base in our creations. While this talent for invention can be handy, it also causes no end of trouble.

Against my typically prudish judgment, I wore a sky-blue dress, snug-fitting and bare-shouldered, to my brother's wedding last year. My friend Logynn, my very own fashion committee, assured me it was divine. When the day came, I girdled and hoisted. At the reception, while I was schmoozing by the cake table, my eight-year-old nephew Michael turned to me and asked, "Are you pregnant?"

I froze. As I squinted at him, I thought, "My God, it's the emperor's new clothes: Only a child would tell me the truth—I look like I'm going to give birth. I need a trench coat. Or blanket. Or tent. NOW."

In the second it took me to have these thoughts, Michael's sister saw my face. An eighteen-year-old beanpole, she said, "Did he just ask if you're pregnant?"

I nodded.

"He asks me that all the time. He wants a baby to play with."

Oh. Perhaps Michael wasn't demon-spawn after all.

1

This is what we do every moment of our lives. Other people say and do stuff, we make up meanings about it, assume we're right in our interpretations, and then act on them. For the most part, this is a ridiculous way to go about things. Our accuracy rate, with this thinking of ours, is abysmally low and it can cause needless anger, grief, and suffering. I thought my nephew was insulting me, my weight, and my own self-delusion. Before Kathryn cleared up what Michael meant, his comment was certainly going to affect his "nephew scorecard." I couldn't believe I'd appeared in public, basically nude. This was a terrible party, never again would I wear fitted clothing, and the nest egg meant for retirement was now slated for liposuction.

Fortunately, in this case, Kathryn was able to short-circuit the story I was creating. Michael's intention was actually a hopeful one. And his question wasn't even about me. It was about him, his hopes, and his world. Rather than appreciating his longing for a playmate, I got mad at him. All this because I assumed I knew what he meant. His personal dictionary and mine were so different that even with the same sentence we were headed down completely separate paths of meaning.

Thus, the problem. On the one hand, we've got fabulous capacities for streamlining information and interpreting the world quickly so we can move successfully from point A to point B. However, as in the example with my nephew, this process is also fraught with peril.

How We Make Sense of the World

In short, stuff happens. You see and hear some of it. From these observations, you create a meaning for what you've witnessed. Then you make a decision about the other people involved, or yourself, or both—you conclude how someone is, or how things are. Next you take action based on the conclusion you've reached. This process works well for many, many situations.

For example, you want to cross the street. You look to your left and see, say, a large truck speeding toward the intersection. Even though the light has turned for you to walk, you can tell that the truck is traveling too fast to stop. You remain on the sidewalk and avoid being hit. Your thinking process has allowed you to assess the situation quickly and to take appropriate action. Even more amazing is that we can count on our brains to do much of this work for us *automatically*.

Our facility for making sense of the world has been a large part of our success on the planet (that and opposable thumbs). Our thinking processes do take some shortcuts to save time, but—for the most part—work brilliantly for us. We are exceptionally talented in learning, experimentation, creation, and change. Our capacities for rational thought and emotional experience have allowed us to become a species that has created democracy, Venice, heart transplants, existentialism, and Chia Pets.

The workings of our minds are marvelous and efficient meaning-making programs in action. We translate, in millisecond flashes, what's going on around us every moment of every day. Indeed, we cannot live our lives without attempting to figure out what is happening. This expertise of ours is a kind of automatic thinking—thinking which relies on what we already know to define the current moment.

Automatic thinking is highly functional; it does its thing without our even paying attention. Thus, we can count on it to help us recognize a carrot, identify a voice, or ride a bike. We immediately know who that person is in the blue uniform who's putting catalogs in the mailbox. This kind of thinking is our everyday automatic pilot mode of figuring out, as fast as possible, what's going on in the world; it usually works well for us. That's the good news. But, my nephew's question about my providing him with a cousin is a stark reminder: The interpretive process that we call thinking is vulnerable to mistakes.

The Not-So-Good News

Our brains have a long evolutionary history. Fortunately for us, they've grown larger over time adding layers for ever more complex processing. Yet the older parts of the brain, the more ancient elements, have not been left behind. Indeed, our brains have evolved into a set of interlaced networks that interact and affect each other intimately. Paul MacLean, an acclaimed neuroscientist, has proposed that the human brain is composed of three major segments: The first is the primeval reptilian portion, the second is the mammalian component, and the third more recent section is the neo-cortex. His model highlights the major capacities of each part of our brains and the order in which they developed.

At the base of our heads we have the "lizard brain." This area controls breathing, body temperature, blinking—the basics. Physical survival is of primary concern for this part of the brain; it keeps us safe. When we talk about fight or flight, we're referring to the lizard brain. Even though we have big brains now, deep within our neurological makeup we are keenly aware of our territory and anything that threatens our individual safety and power.

The second aspect of the triune brain is the "mammal brain." This is the part of the brain that can emotionally look beyond its own survival. Where lizards lay eggs and take off, mammals give birth to living creatures that need to be cared for. Thus, emotions for bonding and sociability became important evolutionarily for the continuation of the group. The primary concerns of the mammal brain are connection, family, and tribe. Feelings of closeness, inclusion, and love occur here; so do feelings of jealousy, anger, and hate. This is where the limbic system developed—the emotional wiring that has us experience feelings.

The most recent additions to the human brain are cerebral cortexes, which allow for logic and objectivity. This third section, the "learning brain," seeks knowledge, growth, and meaning. Our capacities for reason, abstract ideas, and logic reside here. When there's little to no stress or threat we're in good shape and can hang out here thinking big thoughts.

One of the amazing capacities of our brains is that they work wonderfully well without us. They can just run on automatic. We can breathe, walk, emote, talk, drive, argue without ever involving the learning brain. One of the side-effects of this efficiency is that we fall into routines with our thinking and, quite unconsciously, become stuck in patterns that limit us. We persist in thinking and feeling the same way even when it's unwarranted or makes us unhappy. Through the resulting misjudgments and misunderstandings we can lose friends, lose jobs, lose ourselves.

I call this Rat Brain. For the rat, a mammal with a scaly reptilian tail is a furtive survivor who travels in the dark just like the unconscious, lower-level thinking that runs most of our day-to-day living. Basically, our reptilian approach—kill or be killed—can combine with our darker, fearful emotions to keep life depressing and hard.

Clearly, Rat Brain wants us to survive. Not necessarily to be happy and thriving but merely to make it one more day. With Rat Brain you might have an ulcer and hate everyone around you, but you can beat all challengers at canasta. Rat Brain keeps us "safe" by inducing anxiety and suspicion; from here we focus on being right, blaming others, and "winning." Anytime we feel vulnerable Rat Brain takes over, protects us, and keeps us on guard. And Rat Brain often slips into overdrive without our noticing. It provides us with paranoid interpretations and a fearful outlook—whenever we are pessimistic or disapproving, Rat Brain is on the job.

Therefore, our translations of the world from this perspective can be garbled, half formed, or just plain wrong. We may judge ourselves and other people incorrectly, interact in ways that are not appropriate, and make life and relationship decisions that are mistakes. And we blunder far more often than we realize—it's scandalous really. My nephew asks me one question and I'm ready to write him out of the will, dump my friend Logynn, and my husband too just to prove the point. But because we have evolved—most of us—beyond the Rat Brain we get to choose whether we want to believe our automatic thinking or not.

Fortunately, the solution lies in the problem itself.

Each time we misinterpret someone, we do so in an entirely predictable manner. And seeing that pattern at work means it's possible for us to make far fewer mistakes. For Rat Brain is a default setting—like cruise control. Thankfully, our brains are brilliant beyond comprehension. We have boundless capacities for analysis, generosity, "aha" moments, empathy, compassion, and insight. When we remember this, we can use these abilities to our advantage. Before we can do that, though, we must know how to trap Rat Brain.

The Road to Hell

That January was strangely cold for Florida. In fact, on January 27, 1986, an overnight freeze was expected. Thiokol, a company that supplied parts to NASA, was troubled by the forecast because as the manufacturer of the O-rings, they were concerned about their product's ability to withstand that kind of cold. So, the night before the space shuttle *Challenger* was to launch, Thiokol recommended canceling the mission.

Immediately, a teleconference was scheduled between NASA and Thiokol. Thirty-four people, scattered around the U.S., ultimately participated in this late-afternoon call. As professional engineers, they were used to the demands of this kind of conversation. They challenged each other, interrupted to make clarifications, expressed doubts, and voiced criticisms. However, as the conversation progressed, it became clear that Thiokol did not have a scientifically solid argument for postponing the launch. Everyone, including Thiokol, agrees that their evidence was contradictory, uncoordinated, and inconclusive, based more on intuition than hard science. Ultimately, a well-respected senior executive with NASA, George Hardy, was asked for his view. His perspective was that Thiokol had qualified its product for cold weather and he was "appalled at their recommendation" to cancel. However, he concluded by saying that "I will not agree to launch against the contractor's recommendation."

A few minutes later, the Thiokol representatives asked for some time to caucus on their end, to review their data, and to revisit their decision. NASA, fully expecting Thiokol to uphold its original position, began planning to stop the launch. Twenty minutes later, Thiokol surprised NASA by canceling their warning and recommending that the launch continue as planned. On January 28, seventy-three seconds after liftoff, the space shuttle *Challenger* exploded in a ball of fire. Seven astronauts were killed and a period of national mourning began. The investigation into the technical failure of the shuttle pinpointed the O-rings and their inability to endure cold temperatures as the cause of the explosion.

In order to understand how the people at Thiokol came to such a disastrous decision, we have to investigate their interpretative processes—how they were making sense of the world. And thus, why their actions seemed appropriate to them. For, surprisingly, they were in a fairly typical situation; they were busy, knowledgeable people trying to make the best of a difficult situation. We can learn from their experience for frequently enough, most of us find ourselves in stressful, emotional circumstances where we must make important choices. Costly mistakes—painful, needless ones—are often the result with people we love, people we work with, and even ourselves.

The cause of these mistakes can be directly traced to our automatic thinking. Again, on its own, automatic thinking isn't so bad. When we observe events in the world it's useful to create a meaning for them and then take action that fits what we've interpreted. Much of the time, this is an extraordinarily functional skill. But Rat Brain often runs our automatic thinking.

When we act based on our instinctual impulses we don't always get the results we want. When we assume the worst about other people, we actually get more of what we do *not* want—conflict, anger, broken relationships. Thankfully, the answer is not to assume the best about people—that's not such a great idea either. The real answer is to develop an intimate understanding of Rat Brain. From here, it's easier to see how our interpretations can be off—we can track the links of meaning we create automatically. And we can also see how our actions are based on self-protective interpretation of the world instead of what's actually going on. When this process is clear, we can make more conscious choices about how we think, feel, and act.

Regrettably for the people on the NASA conference call, Rat Brain ran their conversation that day. Diane Vaughn, author of *The Challenger Launch Decision*, reviews what happened. At both NASA and Thiokol, the day before a launch is filled with fast-moving bustle, preparation and double-checking; the teleconference was no exception. Imagine the enormous sea of information swirling around these people—not only the scientific data but all the actions, conversations, and individual concerns that were also occurring. From this vast ocean of information, each participant selected what to pay attention to. Naturally, what each of us focuses on is unique to who we are and what we care about.

The first part of automatic thinking begins here—with all the possible information that we could notice, we choose a bit of data to pay attention to and filter out the rest. Unfortunately, when Rat Brain is involved, we select information that supports the negative beliefs we already have (Part 1 in the figure below). We rarely look for, so rarely find, information that changes our minds or disconfirms what we think we know about people, a situation, or the ways of the world.

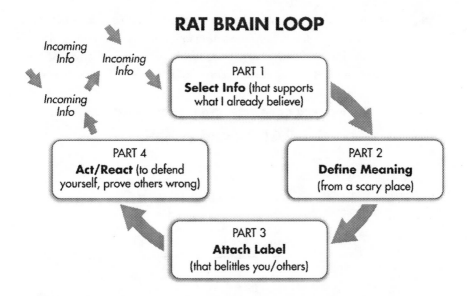

RAT BRAIN LOOP

Incoming Info

Incoming Info

Incoming Info

PART 1
Select Info (that supports what I already believe)

PART 2
Define Meaning (from a scary place)

PART 3
Attach Label (that belittles you/others)

PART 4
Act/React (to defend yourself, prove others wrong)

Accordingly, for most of the teleconference participants, paying close attention to a senior executive at NASA was of paramount importance. He was "appalled at their recommendation" to cancel. That statement is a recorded, objective piece of data. Yet, there were many other bits of information that could have been paid special attention to as well. While most of the meeting participants also remembered Hardy's statement that he would not "agree to launch against the contractor's recommendation," this remark did not carry the same weight as his being "appalled." Rat Brain prefers to dismiss the positive and emphasize the negative.

Next, each of the participants had an internal, emotionally charged reaction to what Hardy said—they felt that he was angry and that he disagreed with them. Most of the participants felt chagrined and upset by Hardy's statement; they were embarrassed by their lack of scientific evidence and Hardy's disapproval. With

Rat Brain (Part 2) in charge the immediate meaning of this event was defined from a fearful, defensive perspective.

Once a meaning is identified, Rat Brain quickly moves to label the competence and motivations of everyone involved (Part 3). After inferring that Hardy was angry with them, many people on the call concluded that he wanted the shuttle launched and was using his senior position to push them into it. Given this pressure, they felt shut down. They then took action (Part 4) that they felt was appropriate to their interpretation of what was going on. As often happens in organizations, they stopped talking.

Comments like Hardy's, and the inferences made from those remarks led people who were against the launch to stop arguing and allow it to go on as planned. Sadly, that was not the response Hardy sought. His intention was to clarify the scientific argument and, at the same time, completely support Thiokol's position.

"PRESSURED" PARTICIPANT'S
RAT BRAIN LOOP

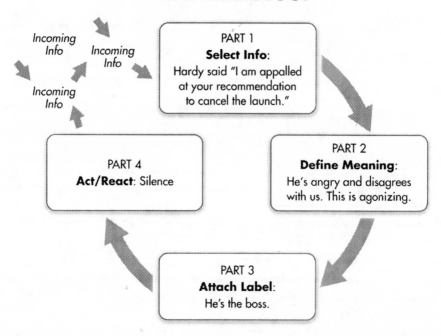

Inside Rat Brain

Rat Brain is exactly the place to start in order to move beyond our all-too-automatic processes of thinking and feeling, to begin to discern that the powerful engines in our heads and hearts often have their way without us even noticing. It's not surprising that we don't notice those automatic patterns in ourselves. Few of us are trained to notice our interpretations of events, to explore our emotional habits, or to trust our own intuition and compassion. That's about to change.

This book is a lever for you—to provide you with some key insights that will support you in changing your automatic thinking. Archimedes said that if he had a lever long enough, he could move the world. With this work, you'll move your world. This doesn't mean that you have to give up your old habits completely. How could we entirely surrender the sensational satisfaction of gossip, snap judgments, melodrama, or blame? I can go whole days in a row where I've forgotten everything I've ever learned about getting over myself. (When a neighbor suggested that my puppy barked too much, I found a doll in that man's likeness and stuck pins in it.)

Wanting to move beyond your Rat Brain is a noble, useful aspiration. And you will do it. Yet part of the human experience is also to backslide, complain, and wish other people would do the heavy lifting. Fair enough; we've got room for that. This is not an all or nothing proposition; you choose when, where, and how often you go off automatic. What I want for you is more choice. Often our lives feel like they are happening to us and that we're swept along by uncontrollable currents. The point here is to see how each one of us is responsible for creating the lives we have, for what we're attracting to ourselves, and even for what we're complaining about.

Once you see how Rat Brain keeps us running in circles, you don't have to do it anymore. You will trust your own thinking processes. With new insight, you can use your heart and mind more consciously. You will take responsibility for the interpretations you are now aware of creating. You can feel emotions more fully because they're seen as simply an experience, not fact.

Generally, people come to this work so they can change their lives, enlarge what's available to them, move beyond the frustrations of doing the same things and expecting different results. Your goals for what you want to be different in your life can range from leading your company through a change, rediscovering your spouse, believing in yourself, or having a richer relationship with your child. Mine was to overcome an immobilizing fear of my maniac boss.

2

The Devil You Know: Thinking

○ ○

Harvey Penick, a U.S. golfing amateur and author, wrote The Little Red Book, *which remains the best-selling golf book ever published. It was written with a collaborator, Bud Shrake, whose agent negotiated the sale to a large New York publisher. When told his share of the money would be $85,000, Penick, who had never written a book before, panicked.*

"Bud," he said worriedly to his co-author, "I don't think I can raise that kind of money."

It was my first real job—real in the sense of big business, big bucks, big work. For me, a former high school teacher, this job was one big deal. After grad school, I had been hired as a contractor for three months with an international technology firm. Ideally, after this trial period, I hoped to be hired on permanently. I had interviewed with my new boss, Peter Drummond, over lunch at a chic French restaurant. His height and bulk had filled the doorway. His salt and pepper hair—mostly salt—was cut short to control his curls. The navy suit he wore was of a silky, lustrous fabric, but he shrugged off the jacket immediately and rolled up his sleeves. I glimpsed a dark tattoo on his right forearm. It didn't fit in with the rest of his appearance.

Happily, though, he had hired me. And now I was sitting in my very first staff meeting eager and expectant. There were five of us in a small windowless conference room. The oval table was too big for the space so when we backed up, our chairs hit the wall. Peter sat at the head of the table near the double doors; two of us were on one long side of the table, two on the other. One of my colleagues, Lindsay brought up what was apparently her pet issue. She outlined her need for an assistant. Peter, in a flat tone of voice, said that we could talk about this topic until noon, but after that we would not discuss it again.

My eyes bulged. It did not sound as if Lindsay was going to be successful and I felt embarrassed. However, Peter's statement did not impede Lindsay or my other two colleagues—they just talked faster. Nervously, I watched the clock over Peter's head as it edged toward noon. I gripped the arms of my chair. The conversation continued. Nothing happened. I began to relax. Then at 12:15, while Lindsay was speaking, Peter stood up, walked out, and shut the door. It closed with a loud click.

The four of us looked at each other. I was shocked. Lindsay picked up the thread where she had left off and continued talking. We all listened, nodding. We didn't mention that Peter had left. We didn't change the subject; we kept going. Twenty minutes later Peter came back in and sat down with a blank face. One of my colleagues brought up a new topic and off we went discussing performance appraisals with no apparent resolution for Lindsay.

When I tell this story to my workshop participants, I hear all kinds of possible interpretations about what Peter did. He had to use the restroom. He was hungry and left to eat. He had an appointment. All calm, reasonable interpretations.

My story had drama: I was sure Peter had lost his temper and had to leave the room so he wouldn't blow up. During the meeting, my stomach was in knots and I wondered what kind of dysfunctional dynamic I had fallen into. Over the following weeks, I was careful around Peter. I kept things light and avoided irritating him. I didn't deliver any bad news and I was as entertaining as I could be. He was unfailingly charming and laughed at all my jokes. Sometimes though, he looked at me questioningly which was worrying. But mostly I felt I was doing a good job of not provoking him.

A couple of weeks after that staff meeting, I realized with a shock, how much energy I was spending on managing what I said and did with Peter. While I wanted an easy-going, fun atmosphere to work in, I found myself constantly monitoring what I should and shouldn't say around my boss. It was draining. I lost my patience with my acting career and decided that if Peter had a temper, I would have to deal with it. Besides, Peter might start to see me as a lightweight who didn't take the job seriously. This was not an impression I wanted to make. As I considered my interactions with him, I could see that the staff meeting had been a trigger for me. It was time to check in with him about what had really happened there. I finally gathered the courage to talk with him about that day.

Here's what I found out. Peter had a phone call scheduled—one that he had canceled twice before and felt obligated to take. Guessing we would break for lunch by noon he had scheduled it for 12:15. He had slipped in and out of the room, unobtrusively he felt, and completed the call. What a letdown—it had been strangely exhilarating to have a nut-job for a boss.

Thinking On Automatic

Now let's slow down the process of automatic thinking. Let's check out each step that's involved; for there are clear steps here. Usually they flash by so quickly that we are not conscious of them. That's how they continue to run the show like a stage manager, behind the scenes. We're going to draw back the curtains and shine some light on them. Once we see how they work, we can decide if we want automatic thinking to be in charge or not.

The first thing to know is that automatic thinking is typically a closed loop—a self-sealing circuit. Much of our "thinking" is like a piece of film whose ends have been spliced together so the same material plays back continuously. We can be amazingly repetitive in how we process the world. We pay attention to what we like to pay attention to and we interpret events and people the ways we usually do. By and large, this means that not much from the outside can interfere with the decisions we make about the people and world around us.

I might think, "Boy, Phil is a dolt," and at the same time, congratulate myself on how perceptive I am about people. Since my thoughts are obviously right, why should I bother to doubt them, or check them out, or pay attention to data that might change my mind? Because I already know what I know, I can continue down my familiar path thinking the same things I've always thought.

This might be okay if Rat Brain wasn't involved. But Rat Brain frequently takes over. He warps and pinches the automatic thinking process. The gap between what is really happening versus what we think is happening becomes ever wider. And our ability to influence the situation the way we'd like to becomes more distant as well.

Information Overload

The first step in figuring out what's going on around you is to notice what's happening in the observable world—what your senses tell you. Data are what you see, hear, smell, taste, and feel. If we had a senso-rama videotape and could record everything with it, we would have an objective record of what has occurred. After all, data is neutral—it does not have an inherent meaning in and of itself. Data just is. It's as close to the facts as we can get before we add our personal meaning to it. Here are some sample data points from the world at large:

THE WORLD AT LARGE ACCORDING TO THE FIVE SENSES

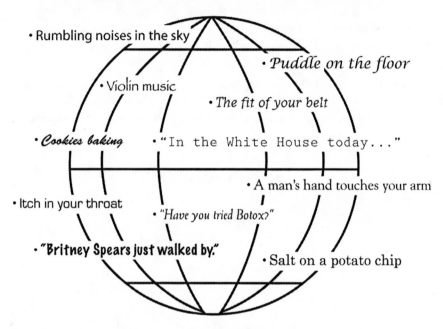

- Rumbling noises in the sky
- *Puddle on the floor*
- Violin music
- *The fit of your belt*
- *Cookies baking*
- `"In the White House today..."`
- Itch in your throat
- A man's hand touches your arm
- *"Have you tried Botox?"*
- **"Britney Spears just walked by."**
- Salt on a potato chip

There's an awful lot going on out there. Did any of those items cause you to react? Maybe some eye-rolling or a smile? That's because you automatically make both a logical and an emotional meaning about what you're reading. Your magnificent mind calls up what violin music sounds like, what salt tastes like, what puddles feel like. Automatic thinking has already begun. And because we simply cannot take in all the information that's out there, we filter. There are endless amounts of information coming at us and we ignore most of it. Usually, automatic thinking makes us notice only what matters to us. This then is the first step of our automatic thinking process: Select Information.

Say I go to a New Year's party. Since I'm a fan of interior decorating, I notice the gorgeous velvet curtains draped over the bay windows, the luscious rugs, the fresh flowers in every room. But I do not take in the homemade tortilla chips or the host and hostess hissing at each other. As far as I'm concerned those things did not happen. I only pay attention to what interests me. I miss a truckload of information but don't realize I do.

If Rat Brain joins in, I become more intense. Maybe, from the moment I received the creamy embossed invitation to the party I have been sure that these people are show-offs. Now I'm overtly looking for evidence to support my theory that this couple is pretentious. With Rat Brain as my guide I'm no longer processing information—I'm searching for details to support what I've already decided. The curtains, flowers, and rugs take on a new meaning; they are evidence. They support what I suspected in the first place. These snobs are shallow, and worse—rich.

This is where automatic thinking begins; from the available flood of information, we pick out what we want to notice (Part 1 in the Rat Brain Loop below). Rat Brain makes things even worse—we only pay attention to what supports the negative ideas that we already have.

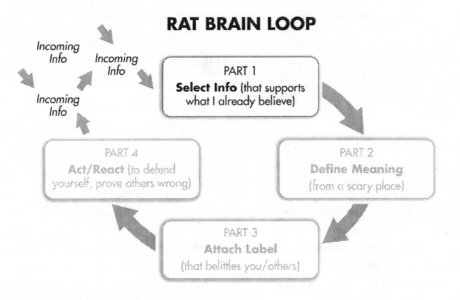

What Do You Mean?

After we've noticed some external data, we shift into our minds. Here, we assign meaning to what we witness in the world at large. Constantly, constantly, constantly we move from raw data to creating meaning, the second stage of automatic thinking. This skill is enormously useful. It delivers messages about safety, like when to cross the street; about pain, like when to duck a baseball; about basic information, like what the word "cupcake" means. Fortunately, we can count on some common understandings between us so that all is not chaos.

Unfortunately, we also have very personal, idiosyncratic dictionaries that we use to define the world around us. I may have a different take than you do on what constitutes a threat, a pleasure, or a risk. These different dictionaries are the cause of most misunderstandings, disagreements, and fights. For these glossaries of ours come from our families, our triumphs, our schooling, our humiliations—essentially, the sum of our past experiences. Given this, it's quite natural that we each have distinctly individual viewpoints on what things mean. And we normally return to these definitions over and over again—automatic thinking.

What's more, when we feel stressed or upset, Rat Brain always makes an appearance. For when each of us goes to our internal dictionary we are looking up at least two things. One is the logical definition of what is happening, and the other is the emotional definition of what is happening. This is actually a false distinction—neuroscientists are currently discovering how intimately interwoven logic and emotion truly are. In *Descartes' Error,* the neurologist Antonio Damasio clarifies how the mind and body are not separate nor are our experiences of feeling and thinking. For our purposes we'll look at them as two sides of one hand; it's important to notice the logical meaning we assign to an event and its emotional meaning as well.

My mother-in-law and I take walks around Austin's Town Lake. Whenever a big dog comes toward us, I head for it hoping to get in some pooch petting. Rosemary, however, veers as far away as she can without falling in the water. As a child she was bitten by a dog in the face. My past experience is that all dogs are sweethearts. What we share in common is that, as soon as we see a dog, we both make immediate decisions about what that means. For each of us, dogs have personal significance.

We human beings are brilliant at this kind of learning, at transferring knowledge from one experience to another. Yet she and I do not really understand each other's point of view on dogs except on an intellectual level. I understand, logically, why avoiding them makes sense to Rosemary, but I just *know*, on an emotional level, that she's really missing out on their fabulousness. That's the truth for me. The truth for her is that I will very likely have a canine-induced scar before I'm dead—if the bite itself doesn't kill me. We both feel, on an emotional level, that our views are correct.

One of the many frustrating aspects of automatic thinking is that it happens below our level of awareness. We feel that we just know what we know, and it feels "right." For instance, I was absolutely certain that Peter, my new boss, was struggling to control his temper. Peter's departure meant that he had lost his patience with our talking about administrative support after the noon deadline. To avoid blowing up in front of us, he left the room to cool off. I was awash in tension and nervous strain—a sure sign that Rat Brain was acting up. And predictably, my emotions around the situation made my point of view feel entirely true. In my case, you might be wondering why I assumed he was angry. Do I have issues with authority figures? Did I mention that my dad was in the military? Rat Brain had climbed into the driver's seat.

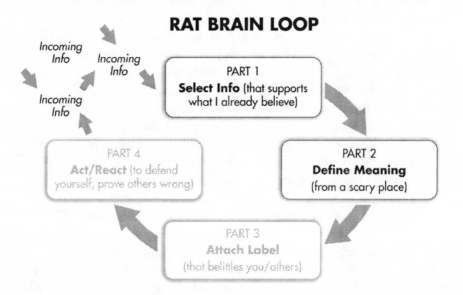

RAT BRAIN LOOP

Incoming Info

Incoming Info

Incoming Info

PART 1
Select Info (that supports what I already believe)

PART 2
Define Meaning
(from a scary place)

PART 3
Attach Label
(that belittles you/others)

PART 4
Act/React (to defend yourself, prove others wrong)

Decision Time

Once we've observed data and defined its meaning, we come to a general conclusion or decision about it. When automatic thinking is in charge, it's as if we have an administrative assistant, a Girl Friday, whose job is to keep information flowing efficiently. Her mission is to make a quick judgment about everyone involved in the situation and then to file it for us. This leaves you, and her ready for the next round of incoming information. This also gives you a clue, in the future, about what you think of different people. Some labels she might use are: "Plays well with others," "Has gun, will travel," or "One sandwich short of a picnic."

With Rat Brain in charge this administrative assistant mutates into a prison matron. She wants to ascertain, with her gimlet eye, the motivation, usefulness, and competence of everyone involved. She's good at short declarative sentences:

"She's a flake."

"He's a sap."

"This is stupid."

She not only makes judgments about others, she includes you too:

"You're an idiot."

Rat Brain favors negativity and sarcasm. After all, R.B. has a job to do—keeping you safe and careful. Generally, Rat Brain assigns characteristics to others, that may or may not really be there, which are designed to make you keep your distance from those suspicious others. It also assigns attributes to you so that you won't become too uppity about yourself either. You shouldn't be out there taking risks, trusting yourself—you could get hurt.

Since Peter had lost his patience in our meeting, I "knew" that he had a temper. Without my even noticing this thinking process, I had come to an important decision about my new boss in less than a second. Rat Brain has a penchant for shortcuts and biases. The only verifiable information was that Peter left the room at 12:15. However, I was certain this behavior was proof of anger management issues.

Another example: You are running a meeting that starts at 8:00 in the morning. Someone who's supposed to be there is not. They arrive at 8:20. Say the person who has come in late is Jane, your long-time employee and lunch partner, whom you feel is a loyal and tireless worker. You assume she's late because one of her children has fallen ill. And being as conscientious as she is, she didn't let this stop her from coming to work. In this scenario, Jane is a hero. You label her a "Trooper."

Now, let's suppose the person who came in late is Dolores, a former colleague who was promoted over you to director three months ago. Your conclusion about why she's late would differ from your conclusion about why Jane is late. With Rat Brain in charge we make up stories about other people's motivations. This is where we fantasize about "why" they are doing what they're doing, from our own perspective. What might Dolores' intention have been from your viewpoint? To have you see how important and busy she is? To have you feel lucky she came at all? Rat Brain is also keen on making decisions about another person's value—like "what has Dolores done for me lately?" Basically, if Dolores isn't with you, she's against you. Rat Brain wants you to decide if Dolores is right or wrong, good or bad, a winner or loser. You label her "Attila."

Simply put, we organize our generalizations around our own interests, our own experiences, what we agree or disagree with, like or dislike.

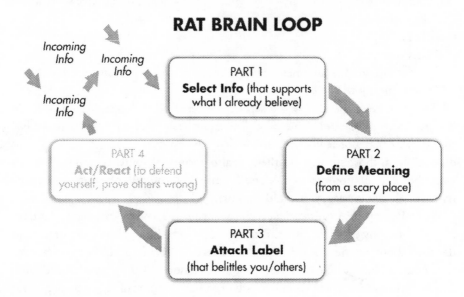

Rat Brain Reacts

So we decide on a label and the gavel comes down. What we do in response to our interpretations includes what we say, our facial expressions, how we gesture, sit, and walk. Action doesn't necessarily mean you leap from your chair; even inaction, immobility, and silence count as responses. For there's as much meaning in a wide-eyed look as ten sentences explaining it. Action here means whatever visibly, audibly occurs—your actions and reactions are the fourth step of automatic thinking.

Let's use the example of when your employee Jane arrived late and you decided she was a trooper. Some reasonable actions you could take: Smile at her as she sits down, ask about her weekend, or thank her for making the meeting. On the other hand, when Dolores, a.k.a. Attila, who was promoted over you arrives late you don't look in her direction, you smile patiently (you think) while she speaks, you answer her plainly and distinctly as if she's slow. You smile with only your teeth. After the meeting, you don't speak with her. Now even if you feel justified in what you did you may have created a situation you don't want. You've begun to distance yourself from her—whether she "deserves" it or not.

In the staff meeting with Peter I kept quiet. Yet based on the decision I made there, I prepared for each subsequent interaction with him; I punched up the positive, downplayed the negative, kept our meetings light, fun, and short. I made certain not to pique his temper with any concerns I had or help I needed. Consequently, I had successfully set myself adrift in my new job, cut off support and guidance, and, perhaps, earned a reputation for superficiality.

The larger point is that the decision you make, the label you create has given you a marker for what you think of this person. Even if you can't remember why you believe what you do about them, you will act according to the label. And the odds are you won't revise or change this label, or any labels you have for yourself either. Again, the mind's efficiency keeps us thinking the same old things. Particularly when our emotions are strong about our conclusion, Rat Brain will keep us stuck in thinking what we've always thought. And since our actions follow our conclusions, our responses to others won't change much either.

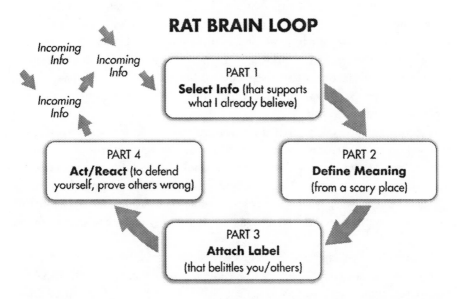

RAT BRAIN LOOP

Incoming Info

Incoming Info

Incoming Info

PART 1
Select Info (that supports what I already believe)

PART 2
Define Meaning
(from a scary place)

PART 3
Attach Label
(that belittles you/others)

PART 4
Act/React (to defend yourself, prove others wrong)

If you happen to have guessed correctly about the whys and wherefores of a particular situation, then bravo. Your actions and responses may make complete sense to everyone involved and off we go on our jolly way. But what if the meaning you created is off? It could be that the label you attached to someone isn't accurate. Yet how we act in the world, depends on how we've made sense of it. Your interpretations directly impact how you act. And if you're off-base, your action may be also. Say Jane was sleeping off an alcoholic haze and you make a point of thanking her for her attendance. Say Dolores has been fighting for a raise for you and you keep canceling meetings with her. Say Peter's legs were cramping and I'm worked up about his temper. Clearly, our responses can be out of step with what is really happening. So we make mistakes, say things we shouldn't, even create what we hope to avoid.

We create a reality we would rather not be living.

Choosing How We Think

For those who are fans of Arthurian legends, *The Mists of Avalon* parallels our current dilemma poetically. In this novel by Marion Zimmer Bradley, there exists a magical place of wonder and learning called Avalon. This is a world where people truly know each other, where learning is the goal, and miracles occur. However, people begin to lose their belief in, and thus the path to Avalon. It becomes ever more separate from them, shrouded in a mist, so it cannot be easily found.

This inscrutable haze is symbolic for each one of us. We rarely find our way to seeing our true selves or seeing others as they truly are. Our thinking processes fog our judgments about how we and others should be. But, joy of joys, we're going to pierce the mist that surrounds each of us—the mist of interpretations, assessments, and distortions that separates us from others. I can feel you frowning. I do sympathize—working on owning your thinking sounds like a good idea for sometime later—maybe.

The decision to view yourself in action, to observe your brain's workings, to choose how you behave and witness your impact on the world is not for sissies. But the rewards are great. Throughout this book, we will discover the good, the bad, and the ugly, together. You may be dismayed to learn that the thinking you rely on doesn't always get you where you want to go. Your thought habits may steer you toward regretful actions, hurtful behaviors, and even make you feel deeply ashamed.

You will also be delighted by your own generosity, your brilliance, and your humor. You are a striving, evolving, yearning creature; you are as fully capable of bounteous bighearted insights as you are of anything else. You are genuinely qualified to create more authentic and deeply felt relationships. You are also hereby authorized to produce the impact you want to have in a powerful, engaging way. You can have all of this.

3

Reality Has Its Limits: Perception

o o o o o o o o o o o o o o o o o o o o o o o o o o o o o o o o o

One of the favorite stories at the Glynbourne Festival Opera concerns Fritz Busch, a German-born orchestra conductor. At his very first orchestral rehearsal, he raised his baton and then quickly dropped his arms to his sides before anyone had played a note.

Addressing the orchestra, he said in his thickly accented English, "Already is too loud."

Maestro Busch is so attuned to sound that even without hearing anything he can criticize it. That's how most of us are when it comes to how we pay attention. We count on our senses to inform and engage us with the world; we want to hear things for ourselves, touch the merchandise, and see it to believe it. From there it's a quick trip to the critique of whatever "it" is. But, we'll get to that later. Right now, the point is that we really have no way to understand the world without first detecting it through our senses.

Our senses are glorious; they allow us to experience the marvels around us. What a privilege to see a spider spin a web, hear wind chimes, smell rain in the wind, touch a beloved face, and taste warm buttered bread. I hear tell that angels, spirits of immaterial substance, stand in long queues awaiting their turn to become tangible sensing beings. The license to experience life physically with full-blown sensation is apparently quite an attraction. We blast music, inhale aromatherapies, and eat the sweetest, spiciest, scariest things. And then there's the ever popular, sex, drugs, and rock & roll. What a kick it is to run right up to the edges of our senses.

Given how we humans are built, we experience a limited amount of what is actually occurring around us. The spectra of light we can see, the pitch of sounds we can hear, are only a small range of what's really available. Yet, we have evolved successfully with the senses we have. So we don't notice, don't need to notice, all the sensations that wash over us. Our senses are miraculous but they do limit us; we rarely travel beyond them.

One of the positive aspects of this boundary is that it allows us to share a common field of understanding. We can generally agree about what red looks like, cold feels like, and salt tastes like. But our senses can also divide us for we have different levels of ability to sense. Some people are colorblind. Some don't hear well. Some don't feel pain. And this vehicle of ours, the body, edits out lots of experiences before even deciding whether to send anything on to the brain for thoughts and reactions. On some level, your body decides what you sense. You are not as in control as you might think.

Even with all that our sense organs can pick up, in no way can we tune into every visual stimulus, every sound, every moment. The amount of sensory information in the world is simply enormous; just watch CNN for 5 minutes. We are afloat on a vast, deep ocean of information; it swirls around us constantly, new and ever-changing, lapping at our chins. Everything our bodies, senses, and minds could possibly process lives in this ocean. With our little fishing nets we try to gather what we can. Naturally we don't catch all there is to catch.

Our five senses are fabulous to have; we think it's a tragedy to be missing one. They're fun to play with, expand into, and test in any number of ways. But what's so surprising, shocking really, is how much we miss altogether. We only receive bits of information and so we hold a highly individual, idiosyncratic, and incomplete version of the world. And let's be clear, our animal bodies are not interested in truth. The body's quest is for survival; this deeply affects what we pay attention to and how.

"Seeing Is Believing" Is a Crock

Tony, the driver of the boat taking a group to Trinidad's Caroni Swamp, frowned at a hip young man kissing his girlfriend on the shore.
He muttered, "I can't stand to see a man wearing an earring!"
Chris, a travel photographer, replied, "Yeah, they make me sick, too."
"They look so feminine!" Tony spat.
Chris glanced at him sideways.

"I never thought they looked feminine. I just think they smell funny."
Tony's head snapped in Chris' direction.
"You think they *smell* funny?"
"Yeah, especially if you eat them."
"You EAT them?"
"No! I told you they make me sick!"

Chris thought he heard Tony say that he couldn't stand to see a man eat herring. This story from Jessica Maxwell's introduction to *Sand in My Bra* welcomes us into the tragicomic world of trusting the accuracy of our senses. I'm sure you have your own versions of mis-hearings that, in hindsight, are ridiculous.

I have misunderstood the following:

What was said: "No kidding, I was annoyed."
   What I heard: "No kidding, you mongoloid."

What was said: "You know that book you gave me?"
   What I heard: "You know that look you gave me?"

Said: "I forgot..."
   Heard: "An act of God..."

Said: "Let's go to a tapas bar."
   Heard: "Let's go to a topless bar."

Once I'd figured out what was actually said, I could laugh. But when I was in the middle of these conversations, I was baffled, certain that the person I was talking to was cracked. It never occurred to me that I didn't hear correctly—it was the speaker who had run off the rails. In some cases it took days for me to realize my mistake. What about the times that I don't know about—where I didn't hear correctly and I think I did? When have I been offended by something that wasn't even said?

Even though I know to be aware that people may not hear well, I forget. If I can hear, they can too. So, I've made some embarrassing mistakes. I've thought I was being purposely ignored. Or I've thought my listener, when just smiling and nodding at me, wasn't too bright. I know it's not fair to judge people this way—it isn't fair. I bring it up to remind us that this is a fact about our sense of hearing that it's useful to remember—it doesn't work that well all the time. Both your own hearing and the hearing of those around you may not be what it could. You, in fact, might be a mumbler yet blame others for not hearing you. Or you might be going deaf and blame others for mumbling. We naturally assume we are sensing accurately and that everyone else perceives the world the way we do. Fat chance.

How many optical illusions do you need to see before you believe that our eyes frequently fool us? And what about those 3-D posters that are a pretty swirl of color until you blur your eyes and dolphins pop out? The word blind-spot exists because our eyesight has a "hole" in the center of its visual field. Smoke and mirrors make us see magic that isn't really there. To put it dramatically, every one of us is partially blind. One aspiring suitor I dated in college lived in the same huge dormitory that I did. He was telling me why he had waited so long to ask me out. I was puzzled. He insisted that I must have seen him staring at me every day in the cafeteria. I just smiled. The truth was I hated my glasses and my contacts were old. I'd never seen him before.

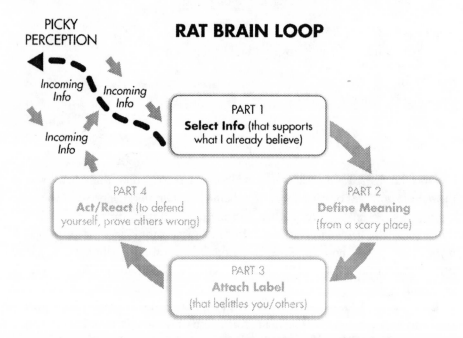

On the other hand, some people have heightened senses. I have a friend who can smell a cold coming on in other people. He says it smells like newly-cut grass. Through the ages, doctors have found that the plague smells like apples, typhus like mice, diabetes like sugar. Then there's the "nose"—a man in the perfume business. While most of us are busy looking, he moves through the world smelling. A magnolia flower, to him, is a lemon covered in gold. He can tell if he's late for work by the strength of the smell of Joy perfume in the lobby. The woman who wears it leaves just before he does in the morning—if the scent is strong he's on time, if it's weak he's late.

Some people are even cross-sensers—synesthetes. They are able to see a sound as a color or taste time or touch an aroma. They describe their experiences in the world like this:

"That phone rings red lightning."

"The touch of your voice is like a brush. Not a brush made of pig's bristles but not as soft as a silk brush."

"This chicken doesn't have enough pointy-ness to it."

These are not metaphors for them—this is what they experience. Consider how we assume others perceive the world with all this in mind. It's dizzying.

I've come to believe that I'm the only one seeing and hearing and experiencing what I do. You may be the only one seeing, hearing, and experiencing what you do. We, each of us, has our own version of what's going on out there.

What Plato Knew

In his *Allegory of the Cave,* Plato makes the point that our abilities to perceive are limited. He imagines most people as living in an underground cave. They sit facing away from the mouth of the cave and are bound so that they can only see the back wall of the cave. Unseen behind them, there is a high wall. Behind that wall, also unseen and unheard by the humans, are creatures putting on a shadow play for the bound captives. These beings have built a fire behind themselves so that the various figures they hold and move over the wall will cast shadows on the back wall of the cave.

This is all the cave dwellers can see and because they have been in their positions since birth, they believe these shadows are reality. But a man who escaped from the cave returns and regales them with stories of sunlight, meadows, flowers, and sky. Yet they are simply unable to believe him. They know what is real—the shadows on the wall—and insist on it to the point of killing their would-be savior.

Plato was detailing the tough job that philosopher's have of convincing people about the beauty of ideas. He was specifically commenting on the treatment of truth seekers, namely Socrates, who had been sentenced to death. But the parallels between the Cave's shadow-watchers and how we perceive the world are striking. We're in the dark, we can't see the truth, and we cling to the validity of what we already believe.

The further we get from what happened, the observable data, the thicker the shadows become. Even when we observe what we think is objective data, we're in Plato's Cave. We make the mistake of believing that we've perceived everything we need to, accurately and fully. We fail to realize that we only have access to a tiny slice of the world at large. We forget that we're limited.

Paying Attention

We can't possibly observe everything. So we're designed to pay attention to what we find personally important, to what we expect, and to what fits into what we already know. Here's an example: In a scene from Douglas Heen's *Difficult Conversations* Uncle Doug takes his four-year-old nephew Andrew to a neighborhood homecoming parade. They cheer and shout with delight as lavish floats roll by bedecked with football players, cheerleaders, and the school band. Afterward Andrew says, "That was the best truck parade I've ever seen!" Given his obsession with trucks, Andrew saw nothing else. Uncle Doug, on the other hand, hadn't noticed a single truck. Each of them experienced a completely different parade.

We are picky about how we perceive the world. What we each choose to pay attention to has everything to do with what we care about. You and I will literally see and hear different things when experiencing the same event. Say, you and I are interviewing a thirty-something man for a sales job. If you are fundamentally interested in positive relationships you might look for, and find, engaging eye contact and enthusiastic energy. But I, on the other hand, seriously care about weeding out idiots. I will look for, and find, hesitations, trembles in the voice, and sweaty palms. Imagine how different our opinions will be about what happened. It helps to remember in this first part of the Rat Brain Loop that we might not have the entire spectrum of what is possible to see and know. That, really, we each see, hear, and take in what we want to, rather than the whole picture.

Eons ago, when I was a sophomore at the University of Texas at Austin, I took a Medieval History class with Dr. Brown. Young and good-looking—for a professor—he had dark spiky hair, a moustache, and round gold-rimmed glasses. He was tall with the slender build of a runner, a bicyclist, or, even better, a yogi.

In class, his delivery of the material was intense. His notes were carefully arranged on his podium but he rarely referred to them. He stalked back and forth on his small stage. Dr. Brown rarely looked directly at anything—not at his notes, not at his students, not even at the clock on the back wall. He would pace from side to side, on his little platform discussing, as if to himself, serfs and crusades and the feudal system.

He was fabulous.

As an ugly duckling for some twenty years, I could detect no signs of turning into a swan. My attempted defense against this fate was big hair—hot-rolled and teased each morning to its ultimate height (to counteract later "fallage")—and loads of make-up. Occasionally, when the Max Factor and Almay and Aqua Net merged together just so, I looked...colorful. I kept hoping someone else would notice these agreeable moments too.

One steamy spring morning, I arrived in Dr. Brown's class a little early and sat down in my usual seat—left side, third row. The professor, standing on his platform, shuffling through the notes he wouldn't use, looked up. Not only did he look up, he looked directly at me. And not only did he look directly at me, he then moved toward me. He stepped off his stage and bent over the front row of desks. I leaned forward, my heart galloping.

Was I about to be cruised by the Professor? How fantastic! What was it about me that attracted him? How should I respond? What would I wear on our first date?

Then, he spoke to me.

"Could you please not tip your Diet Coke back so far when you drink it in class? It distracts me."

"Yes!" I chirped.

You can see from this sad affair that what people perceive depends heavily on who they are and what they care about. My overriding concern was about somebody noticing me; Dr. Brown's concern was about delivering his lecture undisturbed.

The function of this selective perception is to support each of us in sorting through information. This is a highly useful ability akin to your air conditioner's filters—they sort out the dirt, grit, and dust so your cooling and heating system can work at its highest capacity. But you may also begin to see how your personal filters can lead to vastly different interpretations of the "facts."

Gathering Evidence

Many a case study of Rat Brain Loop can be found in the corporate wilds. Here's the scene: The organization is a fine-art museum. They are having a problem with low morale. There's a pattern behind this low morale—a predictable dynamic based on the Rat Brains at work here. For example, a curator is enthusiastically describing an abstract painting to a group of museum-goers, when he catches sight of the guard at the door. She seems to be rolling her eyes and lets out an audible sigh. The curator is instantly sure that she thinks he's a goofball. And he's now clear that *she* is a cretin of grand proportions. Later that day, he mentions her "attitude problem" to the head of security.

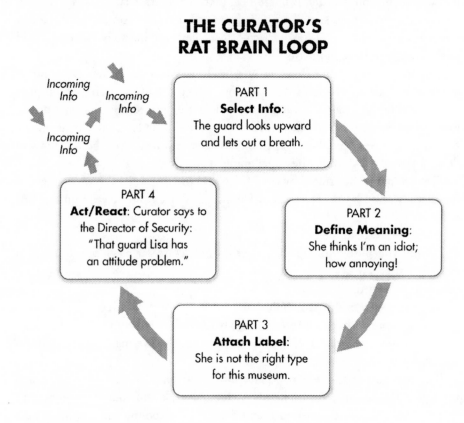

THE CURATOR'S RAT BRAIN LOOP

Incoming Info

Incoming Info

Incoming Info

PART 1
Select Info:
The guard looks upward
and lets out a breath.

PART 2
Define Meaning:
She thinks I'm an idiot;
how annoying!

PART 3
Attach Label:
She is not the right type
for this museum.

PART 4
Act/React: Curator says to
the Director of Security:
"That guard Lisa has
an attitude problem."

Let's make up some other possibilities about why the guard did what she did. Perhaps her shift was over and her replacement was late. Or maybe she had a moment of anguish about her own thwarted art career. Or perhaps she saw Timmy the Terrible Two-Year-Old heading toward her section. Or she suddenly realized she had failed to put on deodorant.

Yet the curator did what all of us do. He took her actions personally, he believed his interpretation was correct, and then acted in a way he felt was appropriate. Notice how the version the curator had of the story was mostly about him. Really, his reaction was probably based more on his own insecurities than anything else. But he feels he has powerful evidence—her eye-rolling. But now the guard has a curator and the head of security unhappy with her. Imagine her frustration and disbelief when she receives a reprimand. This is the kind of cycle of misunderstanding that plays out every day in every organization in the world.

Pretending Not To Notice

The good news is that for the most part we do discern, at some level, changes in other people's energy levels, focus, and moods. The ability to notice these shifts, particularly as they are happening, is wonderfully useful. Being "in the moment" is the goal of many enlightened folk in the world. This is the gift of "being here now"—truly seeing another person, having them feel known, and being conscious of your own impact. And more good news—there's an amazingly rich variety of data available from other people. Most of us telegraph information about ourselves constantly, whether we want to or not.

But here's the bad news—we are shameless interpretative machines. We can't help ourselves from making up stories about what we're noticing. And then once we make up the story that feels true, all the rules of sociability come into play. We realize we might look dumb or rude or off-topic if we explicitly notice what's happening. We've learned how to be polite and not pay attention when someone looks disappointed or embarrassed or bored. Instead, we ignore it. And we get so good at ignoring the instants of our lives that our ability to notice them, as simple data, atrophies.

I was working with some technical engineers who wanted to get better at making pitches to both colleagues and clients. Part of my work with them was to have them give a presentation and see what happened. Here's what I saw. Whenever their audience seemed uninterested (shifting in chairs, opening day-timers, inspecting cell phones) the engineers responded by talking faster, speeding through their slides, and cutting things out to finish quickly.

What's compelling is that these guys were not consciously aware of the attention levels they were getting as they spoke. But as their audience's concentration lessened, they tried to do something about it. While speaking more quickly might have a momentary impact on the listeners, it didn't get the engineers what they were hoping for. So as a strategy, it failed. And yet each of them did it.

There are two points here. One is that the engineers were picking up on the energy around them. But what they did with it was ineffective. They came up with an answer on their own about what to do to affect the inattention and kept plugging away at that even when it wasn't working. And every one of them did the same thing that didn't work. Hmm. The purpose here is not to condemn the engineers, their presentations, or the audience. This example merely illustrates what happens when we send our innate abilities into hibernation; we're not as resourceful or effective as we naturally can be. It's time to get some of this intelligence back.

The idea here is to re-learn how to follow the energy, the aliveness, the tone of other people and ourselves. The question I ask most often when training people in this notion is "what happened, just now?" What I'm asking for here is the data—what's there to observe. Not why did they do that or what's the problem here; those questions all live in the realm of interpretation. Right now we're looking for as objective a version of the information as we can get. This is where we must start.

Whether you are presenting or coaching or leading a team, your ability to discern, in the moment, what's going on will improve your performance—guaranteed. When I'm working with people on this skill and ask them to blurt out what they feel is happening in that moment, to their surprise, they find an answer. They've unconsciously noticed a change in body language, intonation, or attention. What particularly startles them is that they didn't know they sensed anything. Until asked to verbalize it, this knowledge seems deeply buried. So, an important thing to know is that we each come equipped with a fairly decent antenna system. It's just a matter of digging it out from under years of ignoring it. This may even be the same neighborhood where intuition lives and, dare I say it, psychic ability. Just the simple use of the skills we already have—looking, listening, paying close attention.

Just Noticing

The other side of this skill, though, is the part that can get you into trouble. It probably already has. And that is when you interpret what you're noticing, when you put a why to the shift you observed. The danger lies in believing that you know the meaning of what you're sensing. And then trying to manage the issue based on your interpretation. Just like the engineers when they talked faster. Our only real job is to notice that something's changed—not necessarily to do something about it.

All this knowledge that's available to us is an expanded version of what we usually might consider data. We can include here tone of voice, energy level, body posture, eye contact, and the like. But now, I'm nervous—this is one slippery slope. You may have an expectation for how often a trustworthy person should look you in the eye. And you have an employee who looks down frequently. All those books on body language might lead you to believe you know how to interpret these things but don't believe it. How about sitting with your arms crossed—it's wonderfully comfortable. But you're not supposed to because it means you're defensive and closed off. How annoying is that?

We take great risks when we believe we understand, accurately, what things like body language and tone of voice mean. Because we don't—how could we possibly? You know how complicated, self-torturing, and exceptional you are. The internal workings of another person are just as complex—how could we believe that we know why they sit so stiffly or talk so quietly? (Notice how "stiffly" and "quietly" are not the pure data they could be.) The message here is notice everything you can. When you do decide what it means, notice that and hold it as a maybe. A maybe, but more realistically, a maybe not.

We face a daunting task given how much information is available from the world at large. First off, there's too much going on. We are simply not capable of processing it all. So we pick out the things that interest us and ignore the rest. No one has a lock on which data is the correct data—we are each designed differently. This means I have to allow that I could have, just might have, missed something. Perhaps a critically important something.

To add a bit more complexity, remember that each of us is entirely self-oriented—you think it's all about you while I'm sure it's all about me. Hence, we each have a tiny percentage of the data and what I have is different from what you have. Then I run off into my story, into my Rat Brain Loop, about how long-suffering I'm being, or how I'm really doing the right thing, or how I always get the dirty work. And there you are, running off into your story, making up your own version.

We jump so fast onto our Rat Brain exercise wheel that we don't even notice the trip: We are moving rapidly but not really getting anywhere. Typically, it feels like we just know what we know. Our first thought about a situation is generally our last. We assume we're right on our first guess and leave it at that. That strategy might work for picking answers on the SAT. But in the world of relationships and decision making, we could be in trouble. We simply cannot stop ourselves from interpreting, from putting a "why" to the data, from analyzing, and problem solving, and attempting to fix. Indeed, these are among human-kind's greatest abilities. But, because of the high probability that we're off-base, we must observe our thinking in action. And remind ourselves how little we really know.

Here's the challenge: All we have to go on in any situation—to figure out other people, ourselves, and what actions to take—is what is said and done. And yet, not only do we filter out most of what is coming our way, we rely more on our self-interested interpretations than accurate data.

How do we get beyond this? The solution is to pay attention. Sharpening your awareness of what is *actually* said and done can be highly useful. And witnessing the link you create between what you observe and what you make it mean can show you your filters. You'll also realize how your Rat Brain, your opinion of the world, really is all about you. It's not what is inherently true, correct, or accurate; it's the world as you, an entire universe, see it.

4

Forgetting to Remember: Memory

o o o o o o o o o o o o o o o o o o o o o o o o o o o o o o o o o o

A. E. Matthews, a British actor, was performing in a West End play. One scene involved a crucial telephone call, which Matthews was to answer. The telephone rang on cue; he crossed the stage, picked up the receiver, and promptly blanked on his lines. In desperation, he turned to the only other actor on the stage and said, "It's for you."

Our ability to remember—accurately—cannot be trusted. We have incredible memory gaps; if only we could just hand them off to someone else, as Matthews did. Alas, we have only ourselves to dance with in the halls of recollection. Why do we remember some things and not others? Why can a smell or taste or sound prompt a memory which isn't available at other times? Why can I remember all the words to the 70's song *Dream Weaver* but not why I just walked into the kitchen?

We depend on memory, a faulty device, for all that's important—remembering where things are, what we're allergic to, the language that we speak, the formula for the math test, who we're related to and what we think of them. Each of our individual identities are, in many ways, defined by the capabilities of our memory—our sense of self, our intelligence, our competence, our luck in love, our disappointments in life. But the instant an event happens, we start to forget it. We probably didn't notice all the data that occurred to begin with. And the information that does make it through is affected by our emotional state—we may not even register what's happening because we're bored, distracted, or stressed out.

Accordingly, we miss things. And even when some information does make it into our frame of attention it doesn't yet have a permanent home. The temporary storage spot for keeping track of the present moment, when conversations are going on, when events are happening around us is the working memory. This guy is busy all the time, juggling as much as he can for as long as he can. But the deal is he can juggle only about seven items at one time. As more flaming bowling pins enter his path, he has to throw out some tennis balls. He's willing to let in a certain number of items, but they better be good because something else must be rejected. Working memory, with one hand, grabs the latest information coming in. With the other hand, he discards most everything that came before.

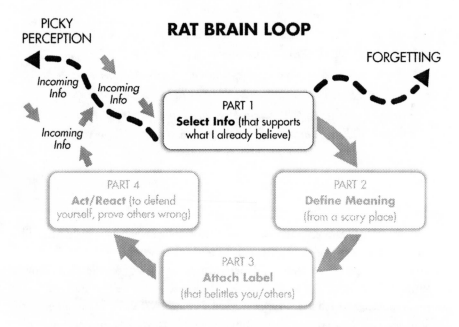

Not long ago, I was working with a group of mechanical engineers who had engaged in a spirited discussion about the meaning of "liberty." Thirty minutes later, when they took a memory test about who had said what, no one got a single answer correct. Not one. Everyone had different memories, not only about who had spoken, but what they had said. Even people who had said particularly memorable things didn't remember saying them. One of the participants, Geoffrey, a barrel-chested man in his fifties, finally announced that he had "no recollection of what had actually happened, only my judgments remain." Like Geoffrey, most of us simply trust that we know what we know. We might recall the reasons why we think in such a way; we might not.

We cannot possibly remember everything, or the right things, or different things—we're built to remember what we remember. Our memory systems do not supply us with strict, dependable versions of what happened. We're usually left with fragmentary patches—a crazy quilt—of moments, both real and imagined. Rat Brain happily supplies us with doctored memories and encourages us to believe they're fair and accurate. How are we to tell, then what is true and what is not? Very carefully.

Random Access

In ways that aren't quite understood we store events in our brains that we've experienced. Unfortunately, we think of those memories as perfectly preserved—snow-skiing for the first time, receiving flowers from a secret admirer, being thrown from a horse. It feels as if we have our own DVD "Director's Cut" boxed set—a movie that can be replayed at any time. But this metaphor is a mistake. Retrieving a memory is a process of construction, creation even, rather than one of simple, objective retrieval. We create the memory at the moment we need it rather than pulling out a pure image or story. Each time we say or imagine something from our past we are putting it together from bits and pieces that may have, until recalled, been stored separately.

In the workings of the brain, memory is not one process in one place. Memory depends on an array of neural activities that converge, collaborate, and arrange experiences—a literal re-collection. The physiological workings of memory, which are just being discovered, are enormously complex and multi-layered. For example, the hippocampus, a small, seahorse-shaped organ that is the catalyst for long-term memory, allows you to recall specific events, like your catastrophic performance in the high school play. If the hippocampus is damaged you would lose access to that memory. Yet you would still be able to learn a new skill—dancing the tango—and remember it. That's because the basal ganglia, located deep in the cerebellum, are responsible for cognition and coordinated motion. If your basal ganglia aren't working, you'd still have your recollections but you may not learn to tango after all.

The Big Daddy for emotional memory, especially of fear, is the almond-shaped amygdala in the temporal lobe. Remember the lizard brain? Interestingly, across all species, a larger amygdala equals more aggressive behavior—the more fear the more hostile, destructive actions. In humans, this brain structure differs the most between the sexes; in men it shrinks by more than 30% when they're castrated (just who volunteered for that study?).

The point remains that the brain has a wide and varied approach to types of memory and where they are stored. The coordination between the different parts of the brain, that must engage simultaneously to create a memory, is complicated and prone to interference.

Speed-Dial Forgetting

Forgetting happens fast. Hermann Ebbinghaus, a 19th century German philosopher, was the first to apply scientific methods to prove just how fast. Experimenting on himself, he tried to learn and memorize meaningless letter strings of nonsense syllables from a long list. Then he would test himself at six different time ranges, from one hour to one month, and note how much he had forgotten. Ebbinghaus used his experiences to plot the Curve of Forgetting; he found the falloff is rapid and steep. This is a core feature of our memories—details exit quickly.

Say you have lunch with a couple of friends. One of them is wearing an unfortunate plaid and his sleeves drag through the salsa; the other, to compensate for her newly blank face (Botox), talks loudly especially about her Chihuahua. For a few minutes, or hours, maybe a day, you'll be able to remember particulars about the lunch. But most studies show that within a few hours you'll have forgotten 75% of what happened. The specifics are the first to go—when the event occurred, who said what, where you were, even who was there. Yet, the most compelling aspects of how we interact with others are the words they say, what we say back, the energy they have, the mood we're in, the silent pauses, the perfect punch line. And these are exactly the fine points that we forget.

Even for personally significant events like marriages, graduations, and pedicures, the particulars inevitably fade. After a week, a memory becomes a dreamlike fragment. Based on these inaccurate recollections we make up stories about who other people are. And these very same people pick and choose what they remember and this is how they decide my identity and yours. Each of us has a partial, self-referential recollection of what happened but we believe we have a complete picture. This is why the parts of events and conversations you recall will be different from what others remember. Attend any family reunion and the truth of this pattern becomes clear.

There are only several thousand problems with how "forget-able" our brains are. One is that our memories devolve to what usually happens—even when unusual things occur. A week later the extraordinary will be blurred into a generic description of what typically happens. Whatever you think usually goes on will be what you remember.

And in the arena of relationships Rat Brain wants you to believe that you remember accurately. That you're right about it and other people are wrong.

Often the past we describe is used to justify our feelings, or to convince someone about our reality, or to have them sympathize with us. We tend to want to prove our version of what happened. Our memory systems are so self-centered, self-enhancing, and overtly creative that we'd be fools to rely on them as arbiters of truth.

The Emotional Over-ride

Emotion absolutely decides what you remember versus what you don't. I have some embarrassing experiences to back this up. Way back in the 1990s, I was chosen to lead workshops for the Coaches Training Institute. These courses are led by two instructors. And it's not as if we take turns—we lead together, the whole thing, like an improvisational game. Once I learned how to lead this way, I was hooked; it's like dancing to ever-changing music.

However, on my very first lead, I was paired with one of the stars of the organization as my co-leader. Rick is a charming, funny, cute, cute, cute former actor. Like I said, a pain in the neck. I wanted to dazzle him. I'd prepared, studied, crammed, and went without sleep for a couple of days—I was all set. When we arrived at the conference room, our saga began. Our box of materials had not arrived, the people who signed up to assist us had canceled, and a huge group of demanding participants was headed our way. We sang, we danced, we told our best jokes. But by the third and last day, we were fried.

That morning, we divided the class in half for an exercise. My group and I moved to one side of the room and formed a circle together where I facilitated the conversation. Rick and his gang moved to the other side of the room where they circled up and he ran their discussion. After twenty minutes, he was finished with his group. In my group, we had one woman left to work with. Rick loped over, stationed himself behind my chair, and shouted out suggestions over my head. As he barked, I fumed. Does he not know who I am? Wasn't I a teacher back when he was swanning around on a soap opera? Has he not read my fantastic, somewhat truthful resume? Does he not know that my mother was a teacher long before he was born? And that teaching is passed down like a congenital disease?

Well, you see how it went. On a break, I pushed up my sleeves and asked him to step outside. All the tension of the past week and the fury of my embarrassment spilled out of me. Wonderfully, he completely understood—he was generous, gracious, and took full responsibility. He also got the chance to talk about how the workshop was for him, his challenges, his worries, the reasons for what he was doing. Feeling better after our talk, we completed the workshop. Our participant feedback was nice ("They're Regis & Kathy Lee!") and off we went back to our separate lives of adventure and romance.

LAUREN'S RAT BRAIN LOOP ABOUT RICK

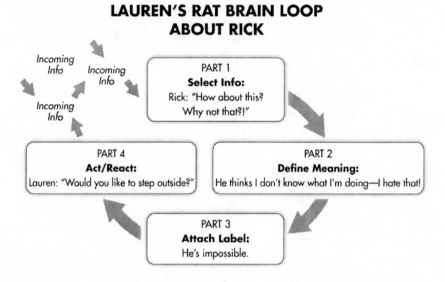

Ultimately my overall impression of that workshop was of having to fight for the trust and respect of my co-leader. As you know, this wasn't necessarily accurate. A couple of years later, Rick and I led together again. At first, I was nervous. But I had much more experience with this co-leading thing and we had an easy relaxed time. We laughed, we cried, we wanted to get married by the end. We left in great shape.

Then we were invited to lead in a huge international corporation—one of those contracts that "if this goes well, we'll be rich and famous forever, but no pressure." He and I, being the approval junkies that we are, were working way too hard to convince the participants that coaching skills were the answer to ALL of their management and leadership needs. This is not in any way how we usually work—after the first day we weren't happy with ourselves or each other. At our debriefing that evening, we both referred back to that initial lead we had where he was insufferable and I had a melt-down.

Then he said, "You know, we led together earlier this year. It was so easy, remember?"

No, I had not remembered. I had wholly forgotten that we had any other experience than that first one. It was as if I had purposely left out any evidence that leading with him could be easy. I was holding on to an old story about him.

And it was the more dramatic, the more emotional one overriding the current, more relaxed experience. Rat Brain likes the worst case scenario.

I Knew It All Along

How we remember events, even whole periods of our lives, says more about how we feel now than what actually happened back then. Our current knowledge and ideas influence, actually bias, how we remember the past. Incredibly, we often edit or entirely rewrite our previous experiences in light of what we now believe. And this doesn't just happen to nitwits; it happens to intellectual giants.

In 1946, the philosopher Karl Popper arrived at Cambridge University to guest-lecture for the Moral Science Club. Popper, author of *The Open Society and its Enemies*, was there to challenge his legendary colleague, Ludwig Wittgenstein, the host of the affair. The stakes were high for both men to defend their ideas particularly because their mentor, Bertrand Russell would also be attending.

This was the first, and only, time that Popper and Wittgenstein met face to face. It did not go well. In *Wittgenstein's Poker,* David Edmonds and John Eidinow have gathered recollections of what became a legendary fight. Yet, even now, the people who were there, all experts in the theory of knowledge, cannot produce a common account of what happened that night. And they all claim to have perfectly clear memories of the event.

Apparently, as Popper was presenting his views, Wittgenstein demanded numerous examples of philosophical problems from him. Popper came up with a few that Wittgenstein dismissed. Then, Wittgenstein raised his voice and waved around a fireplace poker to emphasize his points. He challenged Popper to give an example of a moral rule to which he replied, "Not to threaten visiting lecturers with pokers."

Popper also reports in his 1974 autobiography that after his witty remark, Wittgenstein threw down the poker and left the room, slamming the door behind him. Popper believes that his quip sent Wittgenstein running. Not everyone remembers it this way. One of the eyewitnesses, Gary Geach accused Popper of lying in order to make it look as if he had won the argument. Geach contends that Wittgenstein picked up the poker to use it as a philosophical example while saying "Consider this poker…" Popper refused to listen to him and Wittgenstein gave up. He dropped the poker and quietly left. Geach did not recall a single clever remark from Popper that night.

So did Popper make the joke he says he did? Another eyewitness, Gary Munz, saw Wittgenstein take the poker—red-hot—out of the fire. He gestured with it angrily in front of Popper's face. Then Bertrand Russell told Wittgenstein to put it down; he did so and left. Munz does not remember hearing Popper's joke either.

Another participant, Steve Toulmin, sees nothing unusual happening. He's listening to Popper's ideas and examples. After a question about causality, Wittgenstein picks up the poker to make a point. Later in the meeting, after Wittgenstein has left, he hears Popper state his poker principle: That one should not threaten visiting lecturers with pokers.

Only John Vinelott recalls Popper making his jest to Wittgenstein's face. Vinelott hears Popper's quip and observes that Wittgenstein was annoyed at such a flippant remark. Wittgenstein leaves the room abruptly, slamming the door behind him.

Even with several of the finest minds at Cambridge in the room, the accounts of what happened seem confused, biased, and, at times, in direct contradiction to each other. Some people remembered the joke. But did Popper say it? If so, when? Was it in front of Wittgenstein, or after he had left? Clearly, given the confines of the space-time continuum, only one version of events could have transpired. The sad truth is that this kind of misremembering is typical of all human beings—even brilliant ones.

Did I Dream That?

A common mistake all of us make is forgetting the source of a memory. We can forget which part of a story we heard and which part we experienced first-hand. We can have ideas that feel new and fresh but are actually something we've read elsewhere. Haven't you been in a meeting where you suggest an idea and no one acknowledges it? Then, later, someone repeats it and it's the best thing everyone's heard all week. But you get none of the credit. Rest assured, you're not a weak-voiced ninny—this is the nature of how people forget and remember. (Here's a hint: Telling everyone that you just said that does not endear you to them.)

Often we cannot tell the difference between what actually happened, and what we read, or saw on TV, or imagined, or even dreamed. Recently, I was telling my sister about a friend of Eric's who has adopted three children under the age of 5. As I warmed to my story about this wonderful man, I heard myself say that the children were from Darfur. Wow, this was getting good. But Eric was looking at me closely. Just in time, I realized that Darfur was a separate, different story; I'd seen a documentary. Wait, the documentary wasn't even about Darfur, but Somalia. And wasn't it about boys who were coerced into being soldiers? Yes, they'd come to America but they weren't quite adopted, more like sponsored, and now they were young adults anyway. So what was I was talking about? With such an abundance of tragedy to choose from I'd merged several events into one. Ultimately Eric reminded me that these adopted children were American and their mother had been jailed for running a methamphetamine lab. I wish I'd kept quiet.

Each time we remember, we're adding, subtracting, changing the experience— conflating one story with another, adding feelings, expounding beliefs that may not have been there originally. Naturally, when Rat Brain helps us out we don't notice that we're blurring, fudging, and stitching together all manner of source materials. We are unconscious plagiarists of the highest order. And rarely is this plagiarism for charitable ends; we're interested in proving our point of view, especially if it's negative.

Fun with Reminiscing

Autobiographical memory is a form of creating self. We use our memories to define our personal identities. Designing our memories let's us have a central role in the activities of our lives—not just as a narrator, but as a hero. We want to create rationales for who we are and what we do. We also mutate memories to stay consistent with our ideas about ourselves—that we're good, kind, and smart. Some memory researchers claim that the actual use of memory is merely a process to support the present. We'll create history however we need to in order to support the current ideas we have. It's not that we're evil, lying cheats—we just want to control our pasts.

We share our memories to create intimacy, a bond with another person. Telling on yourself, from your unique past, lets people know you and you them. Remembering together has us understand one another and creates involvement in each other's lives. Because, what we truly want to know, from these stories, is what our friend thought, felt, and experienced rather than the fact of the event itself.

We use our memories to connect—to laugh, to cry, to learn lessons with the people who matter to us. I talk with my sister, Maura, for the hundredth time, about how she sliced up a set of sheets, at age 8, with her new Swiss Army knife. And how our brother took the fall for it. These stories bind us together.

But then there's the other hand. Memories are used just as often to disagree, to disconnect, to shake up another person's self perception or their perception of us. That brother who was punished for the sheet slitting? When Bill was 15 and my sister was 16, he gave her a large bottle of Listerine as a Christmas gift. While they agree on that fact, he remembers this as funny—she does not. Now approaching their 50's, just by saying the "L" word, I get a grimace from her and a smile from him.

With Eric, my husband, I'll wax philosophical about my latest skin-care issue or the on-line sale at Overstock.com and I see him glance down at the newspaper. With this seemingly minor bit of data, his look downward, I come to suspect that he may not be following me quite as closely as I'd like. Thus, I resort to that eternal test of love—quizzing him on what I just said. You see, I can tell how devoted he is to me by how much he can remember. Sadly, he knows nothing about skin or sales. The unhappy truth is that divided attention means that memory suffers. This also has larger implications about all the multi-tasking we do; we don't remember correctly much of what we do or say.

The most frustrating conversations I've ever been in go like this:

"When did I say that?"

"Yesterday."

"I never said that."

"You did!"

"You're making it up."

Unless recording equipment was present, there's no way out. The discussion becomes about the exact words said or not said, rather than what the original conversation was about.

Connecting, even healing, comes about through our efforts to understand not prove. So if I commit to the belief that my memory is the truth, and expect others to buy it as such, trouble is brewing. You may remember your parents as a laugh riot. But according to your siblings, their parents were not funny. Accepting that your memory isn't the only one, or the right one, is the first step to recovery. Too often, though, Rat Brain's need to win is what's motivating us. As my friend Jill says, "Do you want a relationship or do you want to be right?"

Versions of the Truth

One of my favorite memories is of the first time I saw my husband. But how I conjure up that memory and share it with others depends on the reasons I'm telling it. Am I reminiscing with him at our 10th wedding anniversary? Am I talking to my therapist? My mother? My divorce attorney? Not only do we have the physiological challenges of retrieving a memory, we also have a social context for that memory. As Susan Engel points out in her book *Context Is Everything*, whom you're talking to and why will effect how you produce a memory.

Several elements influence how well we can remember something—how unique the experience was, how often we've thought about it before, what kind of mood we're in while we're recalling it. Still, if you've had a good night's sleep, eaten a balanced meal, and are feeling chipper, it doesn't mean your memory will be correct. Even an experience that feels emotionally powerful doesn't make that memory more accurate than any of your others.

In the late 1960s Gary Shaw was a football player on the University of Texas team. He wrote a wildly successful exposé, *Meat on the Hoof,* describing his college football experience. In her harrowing memoir, *Thrown for a Loss,* his sister Cindy Yarbrough, recounts Gary's dramatic rise to fame and tragic fall into adult onset schizophrenia. When Cindy interviewed her father for the book, he described coming home one evening to find that Gary had destroyed parts of the kitchen. He had ripped up floorboards, smashed in louvered doors, and used a baseball bat on the cabinets. Another episode her dad remembered was waking up, well after midnight, to see Gary standing in the master bedroom doorway, clenching and unclenching his fists.

But Yarbrough did not include these incidents in the book; her mother doesn't believe they ever happened. She has no memory of them, no memory of her husband talking about them, no ring of recognition whatsoever. Why not? Did they really take place? Has she blocked them out? Have age and time taken those events from her? Or perhaps, unconsciously, she's rewritten history?

There are some healthy upsides to all the reconstructing, distorting, and forgetting that we do. In the novel *Spilling Clarence* by Anne Ursu, a leakage at the local pharmaceutical plant causes the people in the town of Clarence to remember every moment of their lives as keenly as when the event actually happened. This is not good. One character, Bennie, cannot stop re-running the day, when driving his family to the zoo, the car was side-swiped, and his wife killed. The pain that had begun to scar over and heal is, every moment, a fresh wound. He cannot care for himself or his child in the face of the bloody details of that day.

Memories fade for a reason—several, very good reasons. The present needs our attention. To live fully now, we must let the past go. To maintain a positive outlook on life, we leave behind the negatives. Whether it's smart or not, deserved or not, forgetting allows us to hope.

When I was young, the story of Pandora's Box always puzzled me. Unknown to anyone but the gods, Zeus had fashioned the beautiful Pandora as a punishment for mankind. Before sending her into the world, Zeus gave her a lovely box which he warned her never to unlock. Soon enough Pandora's curiosity got the best of her and she opened it. The world, a paradise of abundance and joy, was now overrun by the demons escaping from the box—poverty, crime, plague, and sorrow. Horrified, she slammed down the lid. But one tiny voice inside begged to be let out. Figuring that things couldn't get much worse, Pandora released hope.

While that may seem like a blessing, my childhood book on mythology did not truck with such nonsense. Hesiod, the early Greek poet, thought that hope was delusional; with no evidence that hoping works and since no one can control the future, other than the gods, Hesiod deemed hope a foolish fantasy. Hope was the worst of all the evils that Pandora released. But now we know differently. Hope and optimism are self-fulfilling energies. What we wish for is more likely to happen because of our attention, expectations, and actions. But hopefulness also depends mightily on our ability to forget; if we remember too well the pains of failure, rejections, and losses, hope cannot survive.

The Eye of the Beholder

For a long time, I believed in my rock-solid memories of my grandfather. I called him "Curly" even though he had broom straight hair. He'd kiss my cheek and I'd rub away the sandpaper feel his stubble left behind. But considering that he died when I was 3, it's not likely that I have my own experiences of him to remember. Ultimately I realized these memories came from one old photo, family stories, and wishful thinking. I've created my grandfather. This doesn't seem so bad—even innocuous. What if my memories also included him as the leader of a satanic cult?

During the 1980s and 1990s, the U.S. was divided by a series of cases brought to trial on the strength of recovered memories. Many of us believe that, at some level, all the events of our lives stay with us, even if we hide them from ourselves, or seemingly forget them. But can we really bury a traumatic memory in our sub-conscious? If such a memory reappears years later should we consider it wholly accurate and truthful? The answer to those questions in the trials of the 80s and 90s was yes. Child abuse cases swept across the country based on the testimony of children who, at first, did not remember any abuse. After some suggestive questioning, they wove fantastic tales of assault, torture, and rape. Many daycare workers were jailed. Another wave of cases raged on as adult children began to accuse their parents of decades-old murders, satanic abuse, and serial rapes. Some of the parents were imprisoned; all of the families were ruined.

Dr. Elizabeth Loftus, an expert on memory, has proven in study after study that memory is porous, adaptable, and gullible. Even when we share a detailed memory with confidence, we can still be entirely wrong. Due, in part, to her efforts many of the mass-abuse case convictions have been overturned and both laws and public opinion are changing about the use of recovered memories. What she saw at work in those trials was the age old belief in the indisputability of eye-witness testimony. A confident witness is incredibly persuasive to us; when people recount their memories with authority, passion, and conviction, we believe. Often, these witnesses thought that they were telling the truth. However, there was no tangible evidence to support those memories. The biggest cause of wrongful imprisonment, by a huge margin, is mistaken eyewitness identification.

You'd think that Dr. Loftus would be immune to recovered memories herself. She's not. When she was 14 her mother drowned, a tragedy that still reduces her to tears. For 35 years she believed her Aunt Pearl had found her mother's lifeless body in the water. At a family gathering a few years ago, her uncle told her that she, Elizabeth, had been the one to discover her mother's body. Until then, she had remembered very little about the death itself. But memories began to assert themselves, clear and vivid, supporting this new version of that terrible day. However, her uncle soon called to explain that he'd been mistaken—she had never seen her mother dead.

What are we to make of our minds? They create scenes that we "remember" as genuine. The neural mechanics that we use for daydreaming, imagining, and inventing, are nearly identical to the processes that lead to the making of a memory. The fabric of memory is threaded with more fiction than fact.

5

Lost In Translation: Meaning

○ ○

Enrico Caruso was a renowned Italian tenor in the early 1900s. A group of reporters once asked him what he thought of Babe Ruth. Caruso, who was unfailingly polite and amiable, replied that he didn't know because, unfortunately, he had never heard her sing.

What was evident to the reporters, that Ruth was a great male baseball player, meant nothing to Caruso. You would think it was safe to assume that everyone knows Babe Ruth but assumptions are rarely safe. This kind of misunderstanding can sometimes feel like a comedy routine—"Who's on first and What's on second." But too often misinterpretations and mix-ups have unhappy results.

So far we know that Rat Brain ignores most information, picks out what to pay attention to, and then promptly forgets it. As if that weren't problematic enough, Rat Brain instantly translates what's happening out there into what it means to us personally. For every incident, we create an immediate intellectual and emotional response—we create stories to explain the world.

This might work out if we all made meaning in the same way. We don't. Every single one of us has a distinctive internal dictionary that we consult when we define the world at large. The exact same information means something different to you than it does to me. The negative interpretations that will grow into great blinding forests start here in Part 2 of the Rat Brain Loop.

When reflecting on why you think and feel a certain way, it's useful to track how you went from an event in the world at large to an instant definition, and then to an over-arching belief. While the entire trip around the Loop feels instantaneous, it does happen in a particular order. There's leverage in investigating this process; it shows how you think, how you link thoughts with emotions, and what your habits are. Knowing how the Rat Brain Loop works allows us to intervene in our own automatic thinking and feeling.

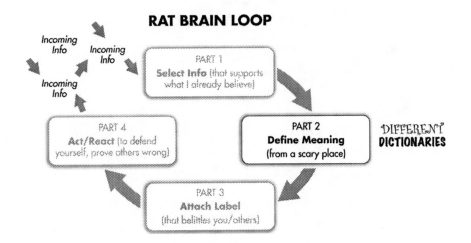

What Does This Mean?

Say that your daughter has her heart set on going to an Ivy League college. She has most of the qualifications, but she needs to ace the Advanced Placement exams, which she took a few weeks ago, just to be considered. After running some errands, you arrive home one afternoon to find her sitting at the kitchen table, the telltale envelope open in front of her. Tears stream down her face and balled-up tissues litter the table. Your stomach clenches, you drop into a chair beside her and sigh. You have a premonition: Old before her time, your daughter ends up living alone in a darkened room with 23 cats. Back in your kitchen, she says, "I did it! I made the scores I needed. I'm so relieved!"

In that example, you may have thought that the exam scores were a disaster. That's an understandable interpretation to make and yet, it was entirely incorrect. We are so good at making meaning out of the events around us that we think we've accurately defined it. Occasionally, we're willing to be surprised by a happy mistake, like a high exam score instead of a low one. But we rarely have such an obvious chance to change our minds.

The personal dictionary you have, like the one I have, is based on anything and everything unique to you. The color of your skin, your nationality, your gender all conspire in your interpretations. The money you had or didn't have, who you grew up with or didn't grow up with, the schools you went to or didn't go to—this personal history affects how you define reality.

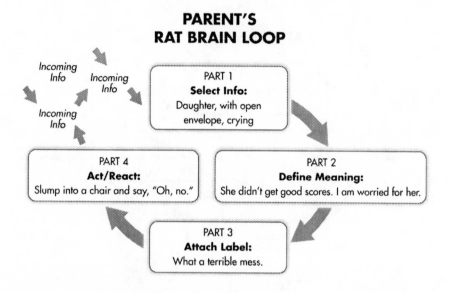

In order to understand the world, we create dictionaries based on our experiences, our temperaments, and our body's abilities. When my husband sees a ball hurtling toward him he grabs it and runs; I freeze and the ball knocks me unconscious. An optimist, I assume I'll recover just fine. A pessimist, Eric suspects I won't. One brilliant friend of mine debates with other people as a sign of respect. His upbringing taught him that this is how you bond, have fun, and pass the time. To me, what he intends as a compliment feels like an assault.

Each of us composes a unique dictionary that's informed by our personal take on everything from politics, to health, to culture, to language. Imagine how many different dictionaries exist just among the people you know. And consider the people you don't know, the communities at play around you, the cultures, and entire nations that stagger on with all their weirdness intact. Why are they weird? Because another aspect of being human is to believe that your way of life is the right one. The dictionary you have access to feels like it's the one everybody should use. But sadly, I only have entree to mine and you only have entree to yours. And therein begins many an unhappy tale.

The Shortcomings of Language

My niece, Kathryn spent a summer studying in Italy. One day she needed to buy a train ticket to Florence. She approached the ticket booth and said, in English, "A ticket to Florence please."

The Italian responded with appropriate pride and gusto, "Firenze."

She said carefully, "No, Florence."

He smiled and said even more loudly, "Firenze!"

She said, "FAH…LOR…ENZ."

He gave her a ticket.

I wish the context of the situation had helped her to understand that Florence and Firenze are the same place. But from her perspective, he didn't understand her.

We might like to speak in the native tongue of the country we're visiting, but learning a new language is awfully humbling. Even in our own language, we run into trouble. We may have standard written dictionaries to consult on the exact definition of words but they rarely help. When we're on automatic, our language becomes sloppy. We use words we don't mean, phrases we don't know, and can end up saying things all wrong. If this weren't challenging enough, let's add more to the punchbowl—tones of voice, body language, and levels of energy. The possible complications are endless.

A friend of mine was nervous about giving a presentation at a prestigious conference. But he was great—confident and grounded. I complimented him; "To me it felt like your feet were on the ground. You were flat-footed."

He swallowed. "Flat-footed—clumsy?"

No matter how I tried to explain what I had meant, I had hurt him. I got my come-uppance though. One day I said to Eric, "I think my mom, sister, and I have the same body type."

"You think so?" he said.

"Yes, a long torso with short peasant legs."

"Your limbs are stockier than your sister's."

"I beg your pardon?"

"You know what I mean—thicker."

"This is not going to turn out well for you."

"You're stronger, more muscular."

"Oh."

How about clichés? Whenever I hear, "the biggest bang for the buck," I cannot pay attention to another word that's said. Before I knew any better I thought it was about firecrackers. Several years ago, I was rather abruptly informed that it had to do with prostitution. Given this unwanted insight, I decided to investigate. The term actually dates from 1954 when it referred to more efficient use of the U.S. defense budget. The Defense Secretary at the time claimed this new policy would provide "a bigger bang for the buck." The "bang" referred to was a nuclear explosion. After that, the phrase came to mean a better value for the money spent. So now when some innocent uses it, I'm distracted by all this and don't listen to the rest of what they say.

For 25 years, my mother, a charming, conservative woman, prepared people's tax returns and counseled them on investment choices. She explained to me that when investing you don't want to "shoot your wad." After I screamed, she asked me what was wrong. For her, that phrase is about overspending. The actual derivation is from betting all your money, a wad, on one roll of the dice in a craps game. Another derivation is from guns—specifically muzzle-loading rifles. In the heat of battle, soldiers often forgot to drop a ball down the barrel before packing the wadding in. So "shooting the wad" was a wasted shot. That's interesting, but that is not what I heard it means. I suggested to my mother that she not ever use that phrase again.

And let's not forget the tired crutch phrases we use to mean everything and nothing: "We'll see," "Let's keep in touch," and "I'm fine." One of the Top 10 worst work meetings I have ever attended didn't start out so badly. I was tired, with that sand in the eyes feeling, nursing a caffeine-loaded drink, and keeping quiet. My only goal was to keep my head up and my eyes open at the conference table. But my colleagues had more ambitious plans for me.

A few minutes into the meeting one of them asked me, "Are you okay with this?"

"Yeah."

"You don't seem okay."

"It's good."

"Well, why aren't you saying anything?"

"Because I'm fine. I don't have much to say."

"Are you sure?"

"I'm FINE!"

And then, because I sounded defensive they became convinced that something was wrong. I explained that *now*, they were right, I was not fine. But that's because they didn't believe that I was fine when I had been.

This is Part 2 of Rat Brain revealed. Because I was saying less than usual, my colleagues inferred that my quietness was about them and the meeting. They were annoyed with me for not being more enthusiastic about the conversation. So my attempt to lay low completely backfired as did their attempt to engage me. This muddle was based on an instant reading of me that was just negative enough to send everyone careening into their Rat Brain Loops.

Basically, most everything we rely on to make meaning has flaws. Our words, phrases, silences, postures can be interpreted in too many different ways. Since we can think far faster than we speak, this gives Rat Brain plenty of time to make mischief.

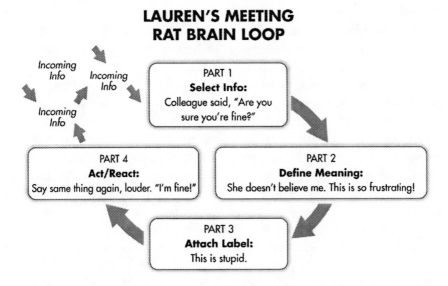

LAUREN'S MEETING RAT BRAIN LOOP

Incoming Info

Incoming Info

Incoming Info

PART 1
Select Info:
Colleague said, "Are you sure you're fine?"

PART 2
Define Meaning:
She doesn't believe me. This is so frustrating!

PART 3
Attach Label:
This is stupid.

PART 4
Act/React:
Say same thing again, louder. "I'm fine!"

Mind Reading

Marie, a beautiful regal woman, was grieving her husband's death. She was also recovering from a recent fall from a San Francisco street car. After it lurched, she fell to the pavement and damaged her face, jaw, and teeth. In *Love's Executioner*, the psychiatrist Irvin Yalom describes his attempts to help Marie manage her pain and move on with her life. It was hard, slow work. In hopes of making more progress he suggested a colleague of his, an excellent hypno-therapist.

Dr. Z. began with a hypnotic anesthetic technique to enable her to numb the painful areas of her face and neck. To Yalom's surprise Marie was a good hypnotic subject and was visibly relieved of pain during the session. Then Dr. Z. suggested that she learn more about her pain and how to differentiate between functional and unnecessary pain—she should begin by discussing this with her oral surgeon as he knew the most about her injuries. Marie looked at Dr. Z. She smiled and nodded.

For his final task, Dr. Z. delivered his presentation on smoking, for Marie was also a heavy smoker and wanted to stop. He emphasized three points—that she wanted to live, she needed her body to live, and that cigarettes were poison to the body. He suggested Marie imagine a much-loved dog and feeding it from cans marked "Poison." Marie wouldn't do that, would she? Their eyes locked. She nodded and smiled.

Afterwards they all agreed it was an excellent, productive consultation. But Yalom was curious. If they each wrote out their recollections of the session would their versions of what happened differ? Yalom was particularly interested in the two smiles from Marie—he had some inside information on those.

First, he talked with Dr. Z. who reported that he was glad to have been a success, especially in front of his senior colleague, Yalom. Dr. Z. saw Marie's smiles, which he remembered well, as proof that the two of them had connected and that she had received his messages. But Yalom had a different take. He knew that Marie's oral surgeon was a long-ago failed suitor of hers. This man was now apparently abusing Marie by keeping her in pain, making sexual advances, and blackmailing her for his expert testimony in her lawsuit against the city. Into this complicated tangle, Dr. Z. had innocently suggested that she talk to him about her pain. It was then that Marie smiled. Yalom saw this smile not as agreement but as ironic—"Yeah, right, that'll be a real comfort…"

The second time she smiled was also in response to an innocent question from Dr Z. "Would you feed your dog poisoned food?" Marie was the owner of a foul, obstreperous creature, Elmer who was the devil in a dachshund. While Marie was ready to pursue new friendships and even romance, Elmer was not. He barked, howled, and snapped at all comers. The living room carpet was the only place he would urinate—no outdoors for him—and the odor was toxic. The elderly Elmer was a full-time job and Marie, literally, could not give him away. Finally she agreed with her veterinarian, daughters, friends, and psychiatrist that it was time to let Elmer go; he was put to sleep. So when Dr. Z. asked if she would poison her dog, Yalom again thought her smile was ironic, that yes, indeed, she would.

Dr. Yalom, in his next session with Marie, asked her about the smiles. What he found out surprised him. Her first smile, in response to talking to her dentist, was actually a plea for the conversation to move on. She was embarrassed that Dr. Z. might know about her relationship with her dentist—she felt ashamed. She wanted to shut down that line of inquiry then and there. The second smile, about the dog, was not what Yalom thought either. While she was appreciative of Dr. Yalom's help, Marie felt that he had overstepped his bounds by encouraging her to put down the dog. Her smile meant "Let's stop talking about dogs. I don't want to make Dr. Yalom look bad."

Even with inside information of the most personal kind, we cannot understand what motivates people. The ebb and flow of emotions, worries, and rationalizations that we contain make for an ever-changing swirl. The meaning I make of an experience will always be different from what you make of it. Each of us is a singular mixture of chemicals, memories, and understandings. To some degree, this makes you unknowable to me and me to you. Most of us don't understand the "why" behind human experiences. There's such a wide variety of reasons for ambivalence, suffering, and gratitude; we can't know the half of it. The work here is not to give up in frustration. But to investigate these differences compassionately, in order to expand the peace in our hearts and in our lives.

Panic First, Ask Questions Later

Up until we hit puberty, most of us trust that at least one of our parents knows what's going on in the world. It seems to be a survival belief—if we can't count on that, why go on? When we become adults, though, we realize they were making it up as they went along. Jeff Jacobson, the author and performer of *Hard Left*, knows the exact moment when he saw through his mother's omniscience.

When he was 8, Jeff's family owned a 1971 mustard yellow Suburban. No sleek SUV here, but a monstrous clunker of a truck. Due to its cranky disposition, the Suburban needed time to warm up in the morning (don't we all?). Because the garage was underneath the family's bedrooms, his mom would back it out of the garage and park it in the driveway. There it could chug away until the family was ready to go.

On this particular morning, as on most, they were running late. Jeff's mom called for him and his sister to get in the car. They went out to the driveway. No car. Back into the house.

"Mom, the car's not in the driveway."

"Yes, it is—get in the car!"

"Mom, it's not there."

"Oh my God! Someone stole our car. Our car has been *stolen!*"

Stunned by the theft, they all started to cry. But their mother managed to dial the phone. She started explaining to the police dispatcher that she needed to report a stolen car. By this time, Jeff had peeked out the front window. Across the street, on the left side of the neighbor's sprawling green lawn stood the yellow beast.

Jeff said, "Mom, the car is in Michael's yard."

Immediately she yelled into the phone, "The Mexicans across the street have stolen our car and are hiding it in their front yard!"

There was a pause, then, "We'll be right there, ma'am."

The terrified Jacobson family, crouching together away from the windows, aghast at the treachery of neighbors, waited. Soon enough, the policeman, the dad of one of Jeff's second grade classmates, arrived with news. He gently reviewed the facts:

1. Several plants between the Jacobson driveway and where the vehicle was now, had been run over.

2. The vehicle had halted in its present position because it had hit a fence.

3. The vehicle was still running.

After this mishap, the Jacobson's relationship with the neighbors was somewhat strained.

Emotional Reasoning

We have a complicated relationship with emotions. We want to experience them—but only at our convenience and in our control. That's why movies, TV, and novels are so attractive. We can plan on what to feel (laughs, thrills, tears), experience it for an hour or two, and then go out for enchiladas. But the feelings we face in our lives are not as easily managed. They can appear from nowhere, be different than what we expected, and lure us into places we would rather not go.

Basically, our bodies are beakers for chemical reactions. All you have to do is eat 5 Krispy Kreme doughnuts in rapid succession and watch what happens to you. Coffee, exercise, Prozac, chocolate, pasta, gin and tonics are all ways that we tip ourselves one way or another. The fun of playing with our chemical balances is how they make us feel—awake or sleepy, exhilarated or tranquil. This is why, miraculously enough, seemingly intangible dimensions of our being can be shifted for better or worse.

It follows that our internal chemistry is really what determines our experience, not so much what's going on in the world outside our skin. This is especially true of our feelings and emotions. These are states that are entirely inner and not tangibly, directly observable. But they're so important to us; there's an ancient belief that our reason for being is to experience as many emotional states as we can. Not just the good or the easy ones, but every high and low, to feel all there is to feel.

Across cultures, humans are born able to feel happiness, sadness, fear, anger, surprise, and disgust. Notice how few of those are positive? Most of these basic emotions are organized around a child's version of "getting what I want." Food, warmth, and hugs equal happiness. Wet diapers, hunger, and no hugs equal unhappiness. (These don't seem to change much over a lifetime.) And these feelings are designed to keep us healthy, well, and nurtured. Fortunately, it follows that parents have wildly persuasive feelings about caring for and protecting their young—logic would certainly not be enough to account for it.

From an evolutionary perspective, our version of genetic material wants to remain on the planet. So our emotions work to help us survive. We're designed, emotionally, to make decisions that are advantageous for us—it feels good to be part of a group, to be appreciated, to be respected. The things we do in order to feel these emotions, lead us to a greater chance of success. It's not that your reproductive achievements would often feel like a conscious motivation for you; I don't go to dinner with my neighbors so that my genetic legacy is ensured. But we are moved by emotions in order to maintain our safe place in the world.

Accordingly, we're also configured to find some experiences unpleasant, especially ones that could endanger us (or our genes). When a loved one spends too much time with someone else, we're jealous. When the boss says "right-sizing," we feel fear tickling our throat. These emotions are the special province of Rat Brain, our oldest, darkest feelings about survival.

As you've seen I don't like to look fat—when someone ventures a comment on weight, mine or anyone else's, I tense. Negative feelings like this can help you realize you're in Rat Brain. The miserable trick of these emotions is they make your thoughts feel important and true. And the more negative the feeling that Rat Brain produces, the more powerless you become. It's so hard to entertain alternative meanings, to be generous, in the face of anger and fear. Dark feelings skew your vision just as completely as when you put both contact lenses in the same eye. And while sorting out the contacts is easy enough, letting go of strong emotions is not.

Passion's Slave

While emotions and thoughts occur throughout the Rat Brain Loop, Part 2 is where they grab you by the collar. The work we need to do here, in Part 2, is to ferret out the initial thought you had and the emotion that's attached to it. Sometimes you can only locate the feeling and not the thought. At first, that's fine—we're born able to feel long before we have language and thought. But eventually it's important to locate the thought as well. Thoughts and emotions build on each other and make an ever-worsening case.

When my nephew Michael asked, "Are you pregnant?" I had both an intellectual and emotional reaction—basically "I look fat. I feel embarrassed." In the moment of that event I couldn't have told you this precisely—I was too mortified. The same is true for the other stories we've looked at. When Jeff's mother heard, "The car is in Michael's yard" what she experienced was "They stole it. I feel outraged." Again, she probably couldn't have said that coherently at the time. We must look at the instant meaning is defined to understand why we believe what we do about ourselves and others.

So, let's look at a specific instance where you've gotten plugged in, wigged out, or hooked like a fish on a line. This is like the "You are here" dot on the mall map—where you are resentful, blaming, mad—"Rat Brain is here." The question isn't whether you should feel these feelings or not—you're going to feel whatever comes up. But how you engage with these emotions is the key. What you need to know is that these murky feelings have a survivalist agenda for us; they are not accurate barometers of the truth.

Do not be enlightened or patient or understanding during the following exercise. We're going into the muck to figure some things out so, no pretending. Also, this activity is for you alone—no need to share it with anyone.

Choose a person in your life that you're unhappy with. After you've narrowed it down to one, consider this: What do you really think about them? From your darkest place, describe them. Are they a traitor? Suck-Up? Imposter? (Foul language may be appropriate here.) This is the short-hand label, Part 3 of the Rat Brain Loop. If you like, jot this down.

A. _____

_____

_____

Now comes the challenging part. We're going to trace where this perspective came from. As best you can, recall a conversation or moment with this person that was emotionally charged—when you were surprised or angered or embarrassed by them. What did they say or do that affected you? We're looking for the data, Part 1 of Rat Brain Loop here. Write out below, what that was.

B. _____

_____

_____

Now, for even more specifics—Part 2 of Rat Brain. When they said or did the above, what did it mean to you? What was your immediate thought about it? For example, "He doesn't believe me," or "She took the credit." And secondly, what feelings came up then? For example, "I feel rejected," or "I feel pissed off." List as many emotional states as you can. It may be easier to fill in the emotion section first and then go back to the thought section.

C. Thought(s): _____

_____

_____

Emotion(s): _____

_____

_____

The idea behind this exercise is for you to observe how your thinking works. This is the key tactic for interrupting Rat Brain—seeing how it takes control of you in the first place. Start by finding the places where you know you're disappointed, doubtful, embarrassed. Then review the specific events that led you to that feeling. What you will learn about yourself is that when certain things happen around you, Rat Brain goes nuts. So when these things happen again, which they will, you have more choice about how you respond.

If you want things to change, it's up to you. And there's lots of power to be had here because your Rat Brain thoughts and feelings are more about you than what's really going on. Your survivalist emotions will want you to hang on to your version of the "truth" no matter how miserable it makes you. This is not helpful. If you're not willing to doubt the meaning you made you will stay stuck right where you are. The important thing to know is that our individual feelings are just that—our individual feelings. They are specifically, uniquely ours. Do not make the mistake of believing them.

Making It Up

Most of what we believe about human interaction is not true. There rarely is a "way things are." Your perspective is merely one of a million different possible perspectives. Knowing this gives us the power to decide what the boundaries, successes, and failures of our lives look like. We, and those around us, simply cannot be proven guilty of being an ass, or a saint, or a mediocre performer. These are merely viewpoints. And they are changeable. That's the power we have over Rat Brain.

This kind of thinking does not lead to anarchy and moral chaos. The context for it is the universal yearning to be connected, loved, and known that lives in every one of us. This is not about abandoning ourselves to moral relativism where anything is permissible given the circumstances. Rather, we learn to understand ourselves and others. If we can brave this path, the result is wisdom.

All there is to changing a habit is noticing it when it happens. Then you can choose to keep your habitual thoughts or change them. I don't mean to suggest that you have to re-vamp how you think about everything. There are some areas in your life that are going just fine and you want to keep them that way. You do not have to re-route every synapse and become a permanently enlightened being—there's the real world to live in. But this is about noticing the places in life where you aren't satisfied, where your buttons get pushed, where you would like to feel different. You get to choose when to look for Rat Brain.

Reflecting on your habits of meaning-making relies on a consciousness of self that many of us forget about, don't have time for, or lose in the busy-ness of life. But knowing how you compose meaning is worthy of your time. Viktor Frankl, an Auschwitz survivor and the author of *Man's Search for Meaning*, points to how our success at living depends on our ability to find significance in our own lives. From his experience in a WWII death camp, Frankl discovered that regardless of his circumstances, man is always free to transcend suffering and to find a meaning for his life. Not only for the worth of day-to-day interactions but for the substance of life-long contribution. Indeed, people enslaved in the camp who couldn't fight off the meaninglessness of their despair and suffering were quick to die. Our survival depends on the ability to make a powerful, useful meaning out of the world around us.

6

Thinking Makes It So: Labels

Jean Cocteau, the French writer and artist, was once asked if he believed in luck.

"Of course," he replied. "How else do you explain the success of those you don't like?"

In Cocteau's joke, we can see a grain of truth: If people you don't like succeed, it's because they got lucky, not because they earned it. We've reached Part 3 of the Rat Brain Loop. This is where we label people. Based on whatever meaning we made in Part 2 of Rat Brain, we then decide who someone is in Part 3. Rat Brain labels include: "Degenerate," "Dumb and Dumber," or "Steroid Abuser."

We relate new experiences and information to what we already believe. If we think of someone as dumb, we're ready for more dumbness from him. This will fit in with what we already "know." If he does something that isn't dumb, it probably won't change our minds about him. If we even notice it, we'll assume it's an anomaly.

With Rat Brain as our guide, we freely disapprove, dislike, and dismiss. We also evaluate (negatively of course) the competency of other people. Our own limitations are fodder as well. The clue for finding these Rat Brain labels is the use of "is," "am," and "are."

"I am so lame."
"She is sneaky."
"They are snakes."
"I'm a pinhead."
"He's an embarrassment."
"They're full of it."

Our brains are set up to categorize efficiently, and here it is in action. But when we label a person, they become like a body in the morgue—a person with a history, with intelligence and complexity is reduced to a toe tag.

The Siren Song of Drama

My mother appreciates a good game of bridge. I do not. I lack the attention span, the strategic mind, and the competitive drive to gamble for a penny a point. Since she retired a few years ago Mom has become *the* bridge hostess. One of the biggest challenges for her bridge club, which consists of elderly widows, is losing members to the never-ending march of time.

Another challenge is keeping everyone sober enough to eat lunch. Mom has begun to serve as much coffee as she does booze to keep the odds 50/50 that each person will be able to drive themselves home. She serves the coffee in her best china cups, which she inherited from her mother. The cups are not only pretty, but laden with memory and sentiment.

After the party last week, Mom realized that one of her six cups was missing. She searched the living room, dining room, Dad's study, the family room, the breakfast area. No cup. There was only one answer. One of these partying card sharps was a thief.

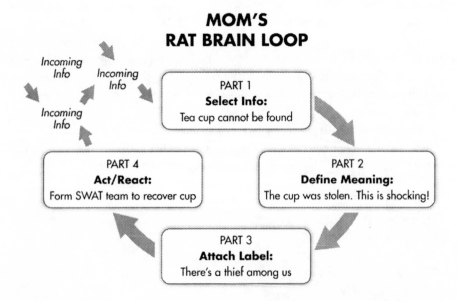

MOM'S RAT BRAIN LOOP

Incoming Info
Incoming Info
Incoming Info
Incoming Info

PART 1
Select Info:
Tea cup cannot be found

PART 2
Define Meaning:
The cup was stolen. This is shocking!

PART 3
Attach Label:
There's a thief among us

PART 4
Act/React:
Form SWAT team to recover cup

Mom tried to remember who had carried the biggest purse. This would most certainly point to the crook—the person who had enough room in her bag to fit the cup. She narrowed it down to a 78-year-old former nurse and an 83-year-old great grandmother. What to do? Could she really confront them? What if they denied it—then where would she be? Maybe she could announce a general "no questions asked" amnesty for whoever returned the cup. Or could she just let it go? No, there was too much at stake.

After a bad night's sleep, she made herself an extra strong pot of coffee to increase her resolve and powers of concentration. Her second cup cooled for too long so she decided to warm it up in the microwave. She opened the microwave's door and voila, the missing cup.

Isn't It Obvious?

Remember the nephew who asked me if I was pregnant? When I heard his question, I assumed he was a commenting about my weight. I also realized for the first time that my nephew was a rude insensitive kid. I did not want this to be true. My own sister's child, my only nephew—a creep.

This brings us to the worrisome issue of how we experience Rat Brain's interpretations; *we experience them as accurate.* Not only are we sure we've interpreted what's going on correctly, it feels obvious to us. In less than a second, I had reassessed who this 8-year-old was to me, what his father's genetics had done to him, and how little time I wanted to spend with him from now on. All of these decisions (Part 3) were based on the meaning I had assigned to his question (which I had misinterpreted). I was convinced that my new assessment was completely correct.

I was once in a course with a woman who began every statement or question to the instructor with "I'm sure I speak for everyone when I say…" After this happened three times, another participant kidded her about being a mind-reader. The next time she spoke up, she said, "I'm sure I speak for…" and we giggled. She looked around at everyone and said sincerely, "Well don't I? Really?" She was astonished that she wasn't actually speaking for all of us. Her experience illustrates the surety most of us feel about our interpretations of the world.

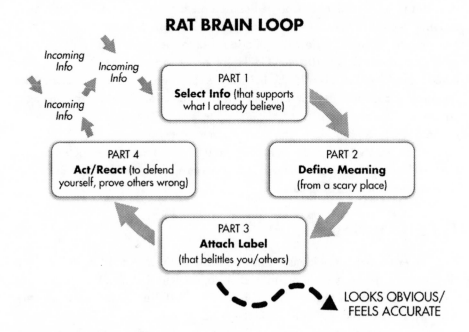

RAT BRAIN LOOP

Incoming Info

Incoming Info

Incoming Info

PART 1
Select Info (that supports what I already believe)

PART 4
Act/React (to defend yourself, prove others wrong)

PART 2
Define Meaning (from a scary place)

PART 3
Attach Label (that belittles you/others)

LOOKS OBVIOUS/ FEELS ACCURATE

Being Right Is Fun

I had held my tongue all the way down to the cafeteria, but I couldn't stand it anymore. At the salad bar, I turned to my good friend Lansing and launched into a story about one of our colleagues.

"You know how Sandy has been missing work? You're not going to believe this. You should have seen her this morning. She was rude to one of our best customers. Unbelievably rude."

Lansing's brow furrowed. "How do you mean?"

Here was the juicy part: "First of all, she interrupted him, told him his idea was dumb. Her face was blotchy and red and she stammered! She made us look bad. I'm amazed she still..."

Lansing stopped me with a calm, measured voice, "Did she say that? That his idea was dumb?"

The wind in my sails turned into a small breeze. Some back-pedaling was in order. "Practically...Uh, I think she said she doubted his idea would work."

Gently, he turned to me, not frowning quite as much. "Be careful how you interpret Sandy right now. I've worked with her for a couple of years. She tends to squash her opinions, but then complains later. She's working on speaking her mind. What she says now may be raw, but she's attempting to be more responsible."

I nodded, embarrassed.

I had known it was possible for people to have different perspectives than mine; it just didn't seem too likely. I was quite the observer of the human species and a good judge of dynamics, motivations, and psychology. My biggest lesson about expanding my interpretive choices actually happened over a sneeze guard.

What I saw that moment shocked me: I was excited about Sandy's appalling behavior. The opportunity to talk to Lansing about her was even more intoxicating. Frankly, I didn't like her much to begin with. This experience had given me more evidence to support my antipathy. What else could I do but talk about her to someone I did like? The point is that I saw myself as right, Sandy as wrong, and I was eager to enlist others in my view of her. I was even bringing in information—that she had been out of the office—that had nothing to do with the incident I related to Lansing. Rat Brain had taken over.

LAUREN'S
RAT BRAIN LOOP ABOUT SANDY

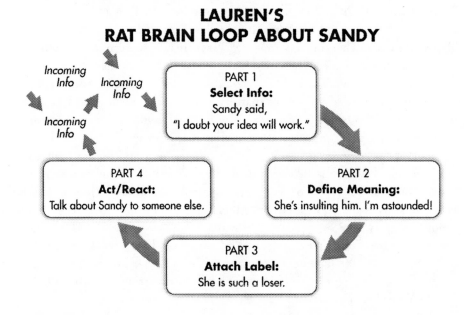

In fact, once I had more information about Sandy's intentions, my perception of her shifted. I was still smarting over how I had misread what was going on, but I could see now that she was being courageous. She was attempting to improve herself. This gave me a different perspective on her than "incompetent weasel." It meant that I could support her, maybe even encourage her, rather than simply looking for her failures.

My gossiping that day changed the course of my life. Lansing, it turned out, was an expert coach in seeing how perceptions can control us. Without knowing it, he showed me my love of gossip and, more importantly, its place in reinforcing the status quo. Do you see the oddly satisfying cycle of interpreting Sandy negatively? Telling others about it? Watching to see more failures that will prove how right I am about what a dud she is? I certainly didn't want to work with losers yet I was dedicated to keeping Sandy in that role.

In no way am I saying that you have to give everyone a chance at everything and be nice to them all of the time. Not only is that not possible, it's not very interesting. Life is about learning, involvement, authenticity, decisions, and action—not mealy-mouthed nicey-nice. Please do not take a "think positive" view of the people in your life. But, on the other hand, do prepare to critically evaluate the negative views you have.

My original assessment of Sandy was that she was an incompetent loser. My interpretation of her, my story about her, was completely made up and more about *my* concerns than hers. Yes, she did tell our client that she didn't think his idea would work. That much is accurate. But he may have been delighted by her directness. He may have known it was a dumb plan. He may have been relieved when she disagreed with him. Or, he could have been angered by her response, her effrontery. None of this means that she was a loser or a winner; it just means that our client also had an interpretation of Sandy, for good or ill. The astonishing message here is that people are not always what we make them out to be.

Some of the judgments we make about others are accurate—not many, but some. What's key here is that we usually think it would be rude to let people know about our judgments of them. Frankly, it would be rude. How do you let someone know what you think about them without hurting their feelings and making things worse? So typically you make a judgment about another person, keep it to yourself, and manage around and away from him. Usually, you'll interact with him as if the judgment were true. This leaves you safe with your interpretation and you can go about ignoring, firing, or divorcing him while he's still clueless about his impact. True change is close to impossible here.

The crux of the matter is to *slow down enough to notice your thinking*. Our thinking processes are so fast that we don't detect how automatic they are. We can interpret an event and react to it without a second thought. The invitation here is to take that second thought, to see how your interpretation of events, and the actions you take based on that interpretation, actually create the world you find yourself in.

Let's look at the literal costs of these kinds of misjudgments. Using the earlier example of Sandy, my coworker who "accused" our client of having dumb ideas, you can see how my motivation to team up with her would be low. I would avoid working with her. I would blame her for those things that weren't completed correctly. Since I believed she was a poor performer, I might even expect us to fail. Not only would I be unhappy with her and my work situation, but also with whoever assigned us to work together. I would be disgruntled, uncooperative, and pessimistic—a good indication that I had entered the Rat Brain Loop. Once I was inside the Loop, I might develop an agenda of proving Sandy's a loser by letting the project fail. And all the time I would be convinced I was doing the right thing by showing the organization it should fire people like her. Sound familiar?

Which Truth?

A 1950 Akira Kurosawa film, *Rashomon* demonstrates the relativity of truth. Set in 12th century Japan, three travelers seek shelter from a thunderstorm in the shadow of an enormous ruined gate. Two of the men, a priest and a woodcutter have just given testimony in a murder trial. They tell the tale of the investigation to the third traveler, a commoner.

The facts of the case are unquestionable. These are the data, the observed, uninterpreted information: The priest testifies that he met an armed samurai and his wife traveling by horseback along a road. The woodcutter found the wife's hat, pieces of rope, and the samurai's dead body in the forest. The sheriff arrested the notorious bandit Tajomaru, when he found him riding the samurai's horse. The sheriff assumed Tajomaru had killed the samurai and stolen his horse.

And yet, what actually happened is unclear. According to Tajomaru, the wife gave in to his sexual advances. She then ordered him to kill her husband because she could not bear to be shamed in the eyes of both men. So Tajomaru murdered him. In his own telling, the bandit appears to be an irresistible lover and a heroic fighter.

"Well, men are men," says the commoner. "They can't tell the truth even to themselves."

The wife does not describe the events in the same way. She testifies that she was raped by Tajomaru. After he ran away, she freed her husband from the ropes that bound him and offered to let him kill her. The samurai condemned her for having provoked the attack. In anguish, she seized her dagger and fainted. When she awoke, she found the samurai with the dagger in his chest. She admits to the murder but has no memory of it.

The commoner allows, "If I believed her, I'd be really confused."

The dead husband speaks through a medium. He says that Tajomaru raped his wife and then begged her to marry him. She agreed on the condition that the bandit kill her husband. Shocked, Tajomaru freed the samurai and asked him what he should do to the wife. She ran away and the thief chased after her. The disgraced samurai then took his wife's dagger and committed suicide.

The commoner realizes that the woodcutter, who found the samurai's body, must have seen the actual killing and demands the truth. The woodcutter claims that after the rape, the wife baited both men into fighting a duel over her. In the fight that followed, the samurai tripped and fell on the thief's sword. Even this version by a "detached observer" comes into question when the commoner accuses the woodcutter of having stolen the wife's valuable dagger. Are any of them telling the truth? Are any of them lying? All we have are glimmers of parallels in the stories they tell. Even the narrator cannot be trusted. *Rashomon* reveals that every individual has his own agenda.

You and I are governed by evolutionary prompts that want us to be successful, respected, and appropriate. Pride and face-saving tactics serve our self-promotional interests—useful tools for getting along in the world at large. They also have us bend stories to our advantage. Tajomaru was certain of his prowess, the samurai of his disgrace, the wife of her misery. These are interpretations, not facts.

The Tyranny of the Negative

A few years ago, my manager and some colleagues took me out to lunch to celebrate my birthday. To surprise me, they ordered a cake for dessert. As I was cutting nice big pieces and handing them around, I offered one to my boss Kay, a slender elegant woman.

She said, "No thanks. Dessert is for fat girls."

After a moment of stunned silence, we broke into whoops of protest. She tried to retract her comment, but we drowned her out with razzing and kidding. We were not interested in her explanations—our feelings were hurt, our ears closed. To me, it seemed like a sour thing to say. The party wasn't quite so cheery after that.

Weeks later, Kay and I happened to talk about our childhoods and she mentioned that she had been heavy as a girl. In fact, she hadn't slimmed down until she was in her mid-twenties. Her mother had always "encouraged" her to lose weight and one of her pet phrases was "Dessert is for fat girls." Kay had been parodying her mother at my birthday lunch. But none of us caught her irony—we didn't have the context for the joke.

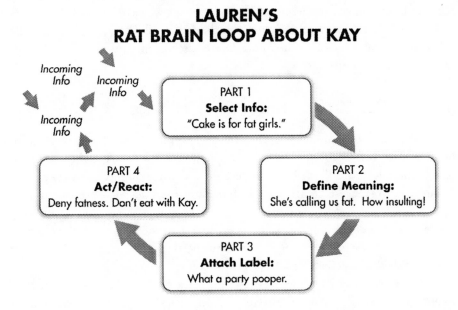

LAUREN'S
RAT BRAIN LOOP ABOUT KAY

You can see how misunderstandings happen all the time based on the smallest of events. From my point of view, Kay had insulted us for eating cake and had become, in my mind, a party pooper. What with the speed of the world and the feeling of how obvious and accurate my interpretation was, I had forgotten—forgotten that I am, that we are each, surrounded by a mist. This mist allows us to catch only bits of information from the world at large. Then, the little that we do observe is slotted into what we already know. We forget most of what is actually said and done, and remember only our negative conclusion.

From that party, I decided that Kay was a wet blanket. I forgot anything else she had said that day that countered my personal story about her. I consistently overlooked that she was the one who had organized the party in the first place. While I could have seen her as thoughtful, caring, and fun-loving, I didn't.

And this is, generally, how we operate. We make sense of the world from our vantage point and are convinced that how we've interpreted the world is true. From an efficiency point of view, this automatic thinking approach really works.

See something, assess it, done. Unfortunately, we overlook a lot, we take things personally, and are certain that our conclusions are fact. Kay is depressing; I am right.

So trusting our thinking processes, specifically in areas where we know we have "buttons" is a bad idea. We filter out most information, we immediately begin to forget what we do let in, and then, believing we have retained all the data and know the truth, we take an action, which may be wildly inappropriate. While this is the premise for most situational comedies, it's only funny when it's happening to someone else.

The End of Civilization

Given that we count on ourselves to correctly interpret the world, there seems to be no reason for us to check our interpretation. It's obvious, right? Unfortunately, this allows a skill we have in speedy decision-making to take over aspects of our lives where it isn't warranted. In human interaction, there are always multiple perspectives and yet, for the most part, we ignore them. You're probably aware that your story about something isn't the only story; it's just the one you care about. Even when you know, intellectually, that it's a good idea to include other people's perspectives, emotionally you don't.

It makes us wonder how we have survived as a species. Once we realize how frequently we are mistaken in assessing ourselves and each other, the impact is overwhelming:

"We're wired to be defensive—how did we ever move beyond tribal warfare?"

"Our veneer of civility is paper-thin."

"I know I do this to others. They must do it to me. There's no way out of this cycle. I should just get better at it and do it to them first."

Given our attachment to the world as a dangerous and fearful place, these reactions are understandable. But the answer to these concerns is this: We can also be kind, loving, and altruistic. The quality of our lives depends upon these capacities. We yearn for connection with each other. Relationships are what we are here for. Part of why tragedy exists is that we matter so much to one another. Our true desires are borne out by every commercial aired around the winter holidays: devotion, tenderness, family, understanding, laughter, safety. As long as this is true, we will continue to connect, interact, fight, spark, and love, no matter how much we get in our own way. Our striving for connection and authenticity keeps us wanting to know ourselves better so in turn, we might know and love others well—or at least dislike them less. All is not lost.

My own experience with learning how to observe my own thinking has given me a way to talk about what matters to me. I used to think it was obvious what mattered to me; it certainly felt as if it were emblazoned across my face most of the time. But it wasn't. This is one of the keys to freedom: What you want, what you think, what you mean, what you intend is not apparent to anyone else. It's important to learn how to articulate what seems obvious to you with patience and generosity.

I wish I could teach you a secret handshake that would make your life easier, your stock portfolio blossom, the champagne and the laughter flow. But truly all the energy that you spend now, blaming, fretting, gossiping, feeling smug, wishing, and harrumphing, will be needed to observe yourself, to notice your judgments, and to hold yourself accountable for them and the actions you take.

You may think I'm asking you to tell the unvarnished truth to everyone and, to you, this sounds like a really dumb idea. I agree. Don't do that. You may think I'm asking you to believe your cousin Johnny isn't homicidal, which as far as you're concerned, is a fact. You may be right about Johnny—get that restraining order. You may think I'm asking you to give up some of your certainty. That's true. You may want to take an antacid.

Fixing It

Frequently, in my projects with corporations, someone asks, "Can't we just fire everyone and start over?" While this joke can feel like the easy answer, to me this is a clear sign that Rat Brain's in charge. Typically, once we have negative inferences about others, we are unable to see much that is positive. Our brains, being the efficient organs they are, generally see proof of what we already believe. It's a big decision to change your mind.

While there certainly are people who are incompetent in the world, our thinking about others can become a self-fulfilling prophecy. Through the power of our inferences, we can create exactly what we don't want. And though it may be easy to blame others for their incompetence, where does it leave us? And them? Not in a very creative, useful place. The fog that surrounds us can prohibit us from believing that people are doing the best they can, that they are facing obstacles which we know nothing about, and that we may, in fact, have something to do with their mistakes.

There are more reasons for pursuing this path of discovery. Most of us, as we reach adulthood, seem to become proud of the idea that we already know all there is to know. It's important to look like we knew what was going to happen all along.

The order of the day becomes a certain detached aloofness. Being surprised, or enthusiastic, or disappointed is not cool. Unfortunately, life in this mindset is fairly predictable, unchanging, and small.

What if you suddenly realized that you didn't know much about yourself and the people around you? What might happen if you suddenly saw that your desire to look sophisticated keeps you distant from the people you care about? What if you gave up the idea that your mother tries to make you feel guilty as payback for your teenage years? What if you believed your talent was worthy of pursuing? What if you knew that your work on the planet was to experience as much connection, loss, joy, generosity, pettiness, and hope as you could?

Seeing both the good and bad in ourselves, owning our perspectives, and shifting them, can cause miracles to happen. Can you hear the trumpets? It's in each of our hands to gather the courage to see ourselves, and others, anew. Here's the thing. Most of us want the people in our lives to straighten up. Working on ourselves sounds as inviting as an audit. But as far as I can tell, looking to yourself is the only way through this. If you ever want those other people in your life to grow up, get a clue, stop pestering you, or to love you better, the answer lies with you. Not them. Wishing that others would change, wishing that circumstances would change, or wishing your luck would change, doesn't allow any of those things to happen.

To make Rat Brain relinquish control, you must begin by noticing who you are and how you are in the world. You are the hero in your own journey here. Your lessons, your evolution, your intelligence in the world, this is your real job. Knowing the way your thoughts work, for you and against you, can give you what a nurturing parent can give you: Room to experiment, forgiveness, awareness, learning, and choice.

7

Louder Than Words: Action

○ ○

An absent-minded British clergyman, William Bowles enjoyed a daily horseback ride. His favorite route took him along a road through a turnpike gate where he had to pay twopence to the tollkeeper for his horse.

One day he passed that way on foot and paid the twopence as usual. The gatekeeper, puzzled, asked:

"What's this for, sir?"

"For my horse."

"But, sir, you have no horse!"

"Oh, am I walking?" exclaimed Bowles.

Clearly, an awareness of what we are doing and how we are acting is helpful in examining how we create our own realities. Up until this chapter, we've focused on what goes on inside our heads. Now we begin to look at how Rat Brain affects our behavior and, in particular, how entrenched our habits of action are, just like our clergyman without a horse. Given that we believe our conclusions are accurate, we engage in acting and reacting in ways that make sense to us. But when we're in the Rat Brain Loop, our actions do not produce the results we would like.

In some aspects of our lives we find ourselves acting in ways that are self-defeating, unproductive, and just plain stupid. The original Latin meaning of *"stupidus"* is a state of being stunned, numbed, apathetic, indifferent, or obstinate. This is Rat Brain territory—when we are moored in the unhappy conviction that our lives have to be a certain way. We think this is the way it is; the way our sister is, the way our boss is, the way our kid is. There certainly can't be anything we could do to shift our relationship with any of them. So, we continue to think, feel, and interact with them the way we always have. This is the self-fulfilling, closed loop aspect of Rat Brain.

One of Rat Brain's most powerful tools is blame; other people are responsible for the situations, relationships, and predicaments that we find ourselves in. If only my art teacher had encouraged me, or if only the CEO wasn't a man, or if only a facelift were cheaper, everything would be perfect. What's so convenient about this is a) we don't have to change and b) we can gossip and complain about everyone and everything that ought to change. This is the art of making excuses—it's also known as Happy Hour. While these activities can be hugely entertaining, nothing really changes.

Insanity has been defined as "doing the same thing over and over again expecting different results." If this is so, most of us are certifiable. We frequently continue to act in the same ways thinking, "This should work." And, of course, it doesn't. The action you take is usually related far more to your Rat Brain than anything useful. And Rat Brain launches us into action automatically. For instance, the way I was acting with my new boss Peter—censoring bad news—was an unconscious reflex reaction. The same is true of being mad at my nephew for insinuating that I am a "lardo." My actions were automatic and all about me. Indeed, each of us lives and interacts in a world of our own.

Crazy Making Activities

When a loved one leaves the room and shuts the door loudly, what is your first thought? Whenever I hear a door "slam," I think the perpetrator is mad at me—for no good reason, either. So suddenly, I'm in a huff. I might act hurt or I might chase him down or maybe I rise above it. But I'm certainly the injured party here. See how quickly the louder-than-usual door closing becomes about me?

And depending on my interpretation, a wide variety of actions are possible. For instance, what if I decided the door had slipped from his grasp? I would shrug off his clumsiness. Or what if I figured the cat was trying to sneak into a forbidden room? I might be grateful he had shut the door fast and hard. Or what if I thought a draft had caught the door? I might check to see if any windows were open that shouldn't be. You can see how the meanings we choose govern our actions. Our behaviors can look sensible or vaguely nutty, depending on what's actually going on.

Most of the Rat Brain Loop happens inside our heads where, fortunately or unfortunately, we spend most of our time. Frankly, as one joke puts it, our minds are like a bad neighborhood; don't go in there alone. And, typically, what happens in your mind is automatic, unnoticed, and feels accurate. Naturally then, we feel we don't need to check anything out. So we have a closed-loop system here that's rarely examined for faults. Thus, believing we've read a situation accurately, we take action (Part 4 of Rat Brain) that seems appropriate to our version of reality.

One evening last fall, I was sitting at the kitchen table with my husband. We had just finished an early dinner. After telling me about his "okay" day, Eric slumped his shoulders and looked down at the table. I stood up and almost shouted, "Let's go out for a movie."

LAUREN'S RAT BRAIN LOOP ABOUT "THE OKAY DAY"

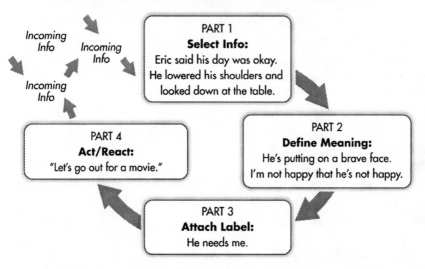

What had happened? In the space of a moment, I had diagnosed what was wrong with Eric. He was putting on a brave face, but the truth was his day had been rougher than he was letting on. He felt defeated and depressed. What we needed was some entertainment, a distraction. Before dinner I had changed into my sweat pants and t-shirt; I was ready for an early night. But this was important. I was willing to sacrifice my own comfort to do what needed to be done.

You can see the saga I've constructed: Eric's the downtrodden victim. I am the heroine who will save the day. The villain is work. This is the three-way plot that many of us live out in our lives again and again. We might change roles occasionally but we've got great soap operas going on most of the time—there are white hats, black hats, and damsels in distress. It's part of life's drama and intrigue. And yet, most of it is fiction.

Frequently, noble intentions drive these epics of ours. We want to help, to fix what's wrong. Of course, it's a fine thing to want to support someone else, but frequently how we try to help is not helpful. Most people in our lives want us to listen to them and discuss important issues with them. But not to tell them what to do—naturally Rat Brain has us offer an immediate fix. "Here's what you gotta try…" Even with an earnest desire to help, my movie suggestion was mostly about me, not Eric. He was feeling bad and I wanted him to feel better. In some relationships, no one can be happier than the unhappiest person in the house. So what does one do in the face of another's discontent? Make suggestions—like going to a show.

After I proposed the movie, I changed into more respectable clothes. I returned to the kitchen to find Eric with his hands on the counter, leaning over, his head tucked to his chest.

"Make it a comedy," I yelled.

He agreed and off we went.

Although the movie was okay, I didn't really enjoy it. I spent most of the movie sneaking glances at Eric to make sure he was having a good time. I even elbowed him in the ribs a couple of times to goose him up. When we arrived home, I asked, "Feeling better?"

"Not really."

I was stunned. My hard work and sacrifice for "not really?" What kind of an ingrate had I married?

"I must have slept in an awkward position last night," he went on. "My neck's hurting."

"Your *neck* hurts?"

"Yeah. I've been trying to stretch it out all day but so far no change."

He slumped his shoulders and let his chin fall to his chest.

"I think I just need a good night's sleep."

Why hadn't he told me this sooner? Why had he let me think I knew what was wrong? Why hadn't he just gone to the chiropractor? Why had we wasted our time at a dumb movie? Then, it dawned on me—I had created the whole situation. I struggled with what to say and settled on "Oh."

Creating What You Do Not Want

When I was in college studying to become a teacher, one of my professors gave us descriptive profiles of several anonymous children. We were to read them and decide how to handle each of them. One young girl couldn't keep her shoes on, couldn't stay still, and was forever putting the other kids together in dances. I sent her to Special Ed. Another child did nothing but stare out of the window and daydream. He never did his homework, failed in most subjects, and was especially bad in math. I sent him to Special Ed. Out of all the profiles we were given I wanted one student—the talented, artistic charmer.

The girl was a pioneer of modern dance, Isadora Duncan. The boy was Albert Einstein who developed the theory of relativity and won the Nobel Prize for Physics in 1921. The genius I had wanted for my class was John Wilkes Booth, Abraham Lincoln's assassin. I hated that exercise. But it was related to a fascinating study done by Robert Rosenthal, a psychology researcher in the 1960s. He conducted an experiment with elementary school teachers and children to investigate the phenomenon of self-fulfilling prophecies.

The teachers were told that their students had taken a test that could predict who would make rapid, above-average intellectual progress in the coming year. The names of the children who could be expected to do well were given to the teachers. Really, though, Rosenthal and his partner, Lenore Jacobson, had randomly picked these names from the class list. The test was a standard IQ test and did not identify "academic bloomers" as the teachers were told. So any differences between these children and the rest of the class existed only in the heads of the teachers.

At the end of the year, the students identified as "bloomers" had greater increases in their IQs than the other children. The teachers also indicated that these "special" students were better behaved, more intellectually curious, were friendlier than their non-special counterparts, and had greater chances for future success. Amazingly, the teachers had subtly encouraged the performance they expected to see. Not only did they spend more time with these students, they were also more enthusiastic about teaching them and unintentionally showed more warmth to them than to the other students. As a result, the special students felt more capable and intelligent. And they performed accordingly.

This experiment had a positive outcome for some of the school children— that's good news. But what about the other kids? Based on how the teachers interacted with them, they did not blossom. Sadly, Rat Brain usually has us keep our expectations low. Unless someone intervenes (who's smart, from a university, and conducts a test) to prove that other people deserve our positive attention, we do not give it. So our low expectations rule our actions. And we bring about the very results we expect.

We're at the point in the Rat Brain Loop of taking action; engaging in behaviors based on our negative interpretation of what's gone on. In *The Fifth Discipline Fieldbook,* a book of tools for organizational learning, there's a great example of how we create negative realities through our own reactions. Rick Ross wrote this all too common scenario:

> I am standing before the executive team, making a presentation. They all seem engaged and alert, except for Larry, at the end of the table, who seems bored out of his mind. He turns his dark, morose eyes away from me and puts his hand to his mouth. He doesn't ask any questions until I'm almost done, when he breaks in: "I think we should ask for a full report." In this culture, that typically means, "Let's move on." Everyone starts to shuffle their papers and put their notes away. Larry obviously thinks that I'm incompetent—which is a shame, because these ideas are exactly what his department needs. Now that I think of it, he's never liked my ideas. Clearly, Larry is a power-hungry jerk. By the time I've returned to my seat, I've made a decision: I'm not going to include anything in my report that Larry can use. He wouldn't read it, or worse still, he'd just use it against me. It's too bad I have an enemy who is so prominent in the company.

Ross is describing a typical, rocket-boosted trip around the Rat Brain Loop that each of us takes a hundred times a day. These trips happen instantaneously—we're rarely aware of them but they are what drive us to action. It could be that Larry needed to go home to a sick child. Larry could have been embarrassed by his ignorance of the topic. Or he might have simply been bored. But Ross took the leap that turned Larry into his power-hungry nemesis. And now, unfortunately, he will interact with Larry accordingly.

From this meeting on, Ross will avoid talking to Larry, treat him sarcastically, and leave information out of reports that Larry needs. If you were Larry how would you interpret these actions? Unfavorably. Yet Ross will be feeling completely justified in his actions and he will have made Larry into his enemy through his own behavior. He has created his own self-fulfilling prophecy.

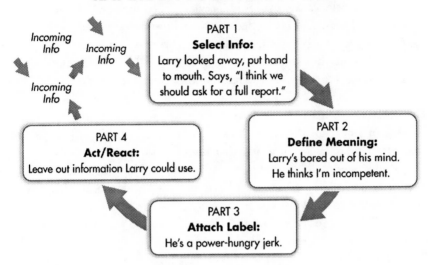

RICK ROSS' RAT BRAIN LOOP ABOUT LARRY

Incoming Info *Incoming Info* *Incoming Info*

PART 1
Select Info:
Larry looked away, put hand to mouth. Says, "I think we should ask for a full report."

PART 2
Define Meaning:
Larry's bored out of his mind. He thinks I'm incompetent.

PART 3
Attach Label:
He's a power-hungry jerk.

PART 4
Act/React:
Leave out information Larry could use.

Feelings, Schmeelings

Our focus here is on behavior—not thinking and feeling. Typically, when you're not happy with the way something is going, the emotions about it feel like the most important part of the situation. And your "rational" mind keeps giving you reasons to feel upset. Unfortunately, these thoughts and feelings can keep you in the same unhappy place. Usually, some of your discontent is due to your actions not creating the results you want. So, while examining the emotions around a situation can be useful, looking at them for a solution may not be.

Here's a radical idea—what if it didn't matter what you felt or thought? After all, your Rat Brain is probably inaccurate anyway—taking action based on it may not be the smartest move you could make. Let's look at some of the reasons for putting aside your private experience. First of all, your internal landscape doesn't have much to do with anyone else—it's all about you. If you can willingly suspend belief in your own stories, you will take more effective action out in the world at large.

Secondly, feelings come and go. An ancient saying, famous for always being true, is "This too shall pass." Now, I love drama, joy, and emoting as much as the next guy but for better or worse, the past is done and cannot be undone. While the past certainly affects us, we can only correct for today and plan for tomorrow.

The reasons for why you're acting in a particular way aren't of interest here; time is better spent on, literally, what you are doing.

One of my favorite cartoon strips is *Calvin and Hobbes* by Bill Watersson. It's about a 6-year-old boy and his stuffed tiger and how they discover many of life's truths. One day Calvin is enthusiastically hammering nails into the living room coffee table. His mother comes running in and yells "What are you doing?!?" Calvin looks up at her, down at the table, and back to her: "Is that a trick question?"

The question "What are you doing?" does usually seem to carry a whiff of accusation, of suspicion unvoiced. Your task here, in this chapter, is to really observe what you're doing in a way that reveals information to you. It's good news that what you're doing could be causing the problem. Because then if you change what you're doing in any way, the problem will shift too. If it helps you to be suspicious of yourself when you're contemplating the question, "What are you doing?" by all means go there. The goal here is for you to see what you are creating by your very own actions.

But before we excavate your behaviors, it's important to decide what you would rather have happening. We're pretty good at complaining about what we don't want. Unfortunately, what you put your attention on will expand to fill your whole field of vision. So it's important to define what you do want instead, to create a new place to go. What would you like to have happening around you? What will you be doing when things are going well? The more specific you can be, the better. And decide on the criteria for knowing that you're getting there—how will you know that things are moving in the right direction? What will be the first signs of progress? And give yourself a break—you don't have to do everything at once—think about small advances. Drop a pebble into this pond and watch for changes in the entire body of water.

What Are You Doing?

If you really want a situation or person to change, you have to look particularly closely at what you are doing. What I mean by "doing" is how you act and what you say (probably over and over again) when you're faced with said person or situation. This could be with your brother who you wish didn't argue so much. Or your son who dooms you to silence. Or your new employee who laughs through his nose.

The first step then is to become an anthropologist observing your own behavioral patterns. You'll look for what and how you do what you do. Your focus is objective examination and description. Not explanations or reasons for your behaviors. You want to figure out how you do anger or do impatience or do sarcasm. Bill O'Hanlon, author of *Do One Thing Different*, offers some pointers in looking for problem patterns.

- When does the problem interaction usually happen?
  (Time of day, time of week, only on weekends)

- How long does it typically last?

- Where does it happen?
  (The office, the kitchen, the car)

- What do you do when the problem encounter is happening?
  (Withdraw, throw things, call a friend to vent, pound the table, eat)

- What do others who are around when the problem is happening say or do?
  (Certain phrases, tones of voice, give advice, blame)

These questions can help you pinpoint the specific actions that keep the problem in place. Once you find any predictable aspect of the problem you can change it and the problem will change. What's liberating is that if you're not happy with the results of what you're currently doing, almost any shift in your behavior will improve the situation.

The key question is "Are you behaving in ways that help you?" You decide whether or not what you're doing is effective right now. This is where your choosing comes in, your choice about what you are doing, calling forth, creating. Each of us is so much more of a magician than we realize—we have power over storms, calm, lightness, and dark. What if we tried on the idea that everything we are happy with, unhappy with, bored by, or intrigued about is all of our choosing? The way we interact with situations, people, our own thoughts and feelings create the drama of our lives. In this realm, there is no one else to blame; other people cannot make us miserable, nor can they make us cheerful. We do that for ourselves.

Doing Differently

Now the fun begins. Once you've decided that what you are doing is not getting you the results you want, anything is possible. The amazing thing about this is that extreme change is not needed. You may think what's necessary is a long sabbatical, or expensive presents, or a lobotomy—not so. Small changes make an enormous difference. What's most important here is to break through your "rational" mind. The things you've tried before probably made a lot of sense to you. The only problem was they didn't work. So now, you might have to be a bit irrational.

Michelle Weiner-Davis, the author of *Fire Your Shrink!*, offers several creative ways to find new ways of approaching situations. A good place to start is to look for what you could do that would really surprise others. Given what you usually do, what would shock them? The answer might be doing the opposite of what you're doing now—a 180 degree turn. A friend of mine, Martin was having a terrible time with some of his workmates. Two of them were chronic complainers and often draped themselves in his office for hours to vent. Martin, a sensitive compassionate soul would listen. And then try to show them the bright side of things. He would point out what was working, what they were lucky to have, how great their jobs were. This only fueled their anger, though, and the conversation would turn even darker.

While Martin really liked his job, the complainers made him want to quit. He and I brainstormed about what he might do differently. He decided on a 180—when either one of the complainers showed up, he would still listen, but he would not attempt to cheer them. He was now in a secret contest with them about whose story could be more dramatic and sorrowful. Martin would outcomplain them both. He laughed just thinking about it—that's perfect. We might as well enjoy ourselves. From the very first time he tried it the complainers frowned in confusion, didn't have much to say, and left after ten minutes.

Another creative tactic to try is "Acting As If" something is the way you want it to be. If you're expecting things to go badly, they will. So the trick here is to act as if they're going to go well. What would you do if you acted as if you liked someone? (You don't have to really like them just act in ways that seem like it.) What would you do if you acted as if this person were the smartest one in the room? What would you do if you acted as if you were having fun? You can choose anything that you want to enact. The odd thing is that after you "act as if" you may start to really feel that way.

Some of the solutions here may sound goofy—so much the better. One of the fastest ways to heal a situation is through laughter. Holding something lightly makes it lighter. For instance, if someone habitually interrupts you, quietly say "Ooga Booga" every time they cut you off. If someone is often argumentative, see how many times you can say "You're right" to them. When a sarcastic friend zings you, respond with, "Great jacket you have on!" These might seem silly but if what you want is to change the dynamic, this will do it.

Another very simple idea is that if you usually do something, do nothing. Don't intervene, don't help, don't advise—nothing. This may be the hardest one of all because so many of us are fixers. But if your supporting, counseling, and lecturing hasn't worked—stop it. You may feel things will get worse if you don't keep doing what you're doing. That's the rub—things won't get worse. You have to trust that taking care of your end of what's going on will have a positive impact. You focusing on you and your own actions can simply take the pressure off. And when there's room to breathe, things change.

Creating What You Want

A few years ago, a computer systems consulting firm asked me to instruct one of their training courses. The program was basically a three-month boot camp designed to improve some of their consultants' technical skills and interpersonal savvy. In a way, the careers of these consultants were at stake. They had worked on converting programs to function after 1999—remember "Y2K"? They helped fix that. By 2000, they were outmoded. The computer languages they knew were now ancient. This program was designed to upgrade both their technical and interpersonal skills.

A group of fourteen software engineering consultants was chosen to attend. They felt lucky to have been invited. Several of them even moved to Austin for the three months. My Home Team, as I liked to call them, had a specific room in the company's training center. Every day, from 8:00 a.m. until all hours of the night, they came to this room to absorb what it was going to take to succeed in their world. My role was to help these consultants with their collaborative communication and work practices.

One day, when they had been together about a month, I arrived after lunch to lead a session. That morning, eight other consultants from a different division, had joined the Home Team's class on web design. Usually when I arrived, all the participants were seated, in their charming, geeky way, ready to begin—they might nod or smile shyly. But today was different. Some huddled in groups and whispered, some sat on their desks, several even stood. They all started talking at once:

"You wouldn't believe those guys, Lauren!"

"No wonder they couldn't get in this program."

"They totally abused the privilege…"

"Their departments better get charged back their part of the cost."

"We let them join us and they were ungrateful…"

Clearly, we needed to investigate What Happened.

"I'm sorry it felt like such a crummy morning," I said. "Sounds like you felt invaded, taken advantage of."

Nods and grumbling.

"Now, you know me, I can't just let it go, right?"

They groaned.

"Remember, I'm completely on your side. You get to do, or not do, whatever you want. Right now, we're just going to look at what happened. Let me check with you first, though, does it matter that you're mad at them? Are there any consequences to this?"

"Well, we work for the same company," Jan said.

"But you may never see them again?" I offered.

"No, it's likely we'll work on projects together," Jan admitted.

"I see. So we ought to take a look—who'll start us off with some details?"

"They didn't pay attention at all!" This was from Erin, who always paid attention.

"How do you mean?" I asked. "What did they do that told you they weren't paying attention?"

"They sat in the back." Mark swung around in his chair to wave at the hinterlands of the room.

"They used their cell phones while the instructor was talking," said Kyle.

"They didn't talk to us or answer the teacher's questions," sniffed Jan.

"Let me see if I've got it," I said. "They came in, sat in the back, didn't talk, and one of them answered his phone during the lecture?"

"Right and two of them were late."

"Okay," I said. "They were not acting the way they were supposed to, the way you wanted them to. In response to their behavior, what did you all do?"

"I gave them a look."

"What kind of a look?" I asked.

Steven shifted in his chair and shot me an over-the-shoulder glare.

"Aha."

"When that guy answered his phone, I went, 'Shhhhhhh!'" said Melanie.

"All right—do we have everything we need? Anything else to include? Then our first step is to gather up all the unhappiness you have about this morning. You do get to keep it but for 15 minutes we're going to put it away. For those of you with an appendix please put the feelings in there. Everyone else put the unhappiness in your left elbow. Okay, now it's time for some curiosity and, if we need it, generosity. From this place, let's walk through this morning. What part did you play in creating it exactly as it occurred?"

Silence.

"Now, it might help to remember that we're just pretending, simply conducting an experiment. It's not like it's true that you created this morning but we're trying on the idea to see what we might discover. For instance, why do you think your visitors sat in the back?"

Steven laughed. "Because we had all the seats in the front."

More silence. A few frowns.

Finally: "There wasn't anywhere else to sit," said Mark. "And, really, why would they get close to us? They don't know us."

"Right, they're guests here. They might have felt uncomfortable," I said.

"I hate to say this," Melanie said, "but another person went outside to answer his phone."

Joanna suggested, "He might have sat on the back row so he could leave quickly. To not bother us."

I said, "Now you don't want to start thinking too generously about these guys. They did ruin your morning after all."

A few feeble laughs—faked for my benefit.

"Let's keep going. They didn't interact with you. How could you have created that?"

"We didn't talk to them," Mark said. "Here we are, the chosen ones, we know each other and this room better than we ever wanted to. It's our turf. And we pretty much just looked at them as they came in."

"Uh huh. After they sat down, what was their experience?"

"Our backs. Until I glared at them," said Steven.

"Or me shushing them," mumbled Melanie.

"What are you noticing now?" I asked.

Joanna shook her head. "We know how to act in this room. Pay complete attention, participate, no phones. That all really works. We were expecting those guys to know the rules."

"Yeah, and they're coming back tomorrow," croaked Erin.

"How do you want tomorrow to be?" I asked.

"The opposite of today," said Mark.

"Okay," I started, "you can see that you may have had an impact on them and the way they behaved. In our hypothetical experiment, if you were responsible for today, you can be responsible for tomorrow too. How can you make tomorrow, without telling them about your feelings, more fun for all of you?"

We discussed some options and I was tickled at how excited they became. It was as if they were planning a surprise party. Ultimately, the Home Team decided to act as hosts. They rearranged the room so that the visitors were interspersed between them. When the guests arrived the next day, they were to be met by their host, welcomed, shown where the coffee and snacks were, and their new seats.

That afternoon, when I arrived for my session with the group, I received a much different report than I had the day before. The morning had been easy and satisfying. These old hands were proud of themselves for creating a friendlier, more welcoming atmosphere. The visitors had turned out to be not so bad—they had interacted in class and added insights to the discussions. And sure enough, several months after that web design workshop, three of the Home Team members were assigned to a big project with two of the visitors.

Peace Is Boring

Happily, this interaction turned out constructively—but only because the Home Team became conscious of what they were creating. Let's review the process they went through before I ruined their fun. To begin, this group had selected data that supported their conclusion about the visiting consultants. The Home Team felt utterly justified in their belief about the asinine nature of the other group. They presented data to me that proved they were right about this belief. They also left out data. Not necessarily in a mean-spirited way, but in the age-old way of thinking—"Here's my argument and I'm going to make it as good as I can." This group was about to get locked into a "truth."

It would be nice if we didn't compartmentalize people this way, but our minds are organized to do just that. We are wired to categorize, make sense of, and rationalize the world at large. Typically, this is our survival instinct at work. The seemingly safe bet is to believe that the enemy is over there, to buy in to the idea of the quintessential "they." This might be a fine way to view things—if it worked. But what it leads to, usually, is escalating suspicion and defensiveness.

The frightening fact is that we actually create who other people are—we create them in our heads. Anais Nin, the author, said that, "We don't see things as they are, we see them as we are." This is where my Home Team consultants interrupted their own typical pattern. They decided to stop blaming others and take responsibility for what was happening. Each of us has a tremendous amount of choice here—we get to see how we are creating what we don't want. One more time—be careful of creating what you don't want. You can examine Rat Brain's impact on your behaviors and choose to do something else.

Here's something else to notice: Didn't the resolution of the problem seem anti-climactic? Everyone got along. The meeting went smoothly. Big Deal. Problems are more exciting than solutions. When conflict appears, there are sides to root for, bombs to defuse, spying to be done, gossip to be had, suffering, close calls, and saving the day.

There are plenty of ways, mostly legal, to get a rush of adrenalin—bungee jumping, open mike night, streaking. It also takes enormous courage and nerve to talk about what really matters. Figuring out how you are the problem is compelling detective work. And discovering how you are also the solution is like receiving an anonymous Valentine card—thrilling, embarrassing, satisfying. You get to keep all the drama and excitement you have with problems. But now these feelings can be directed toward a constructive outcome rather than the same old stories of indignation and blame. Or you can keep company with Mark Twain who said, "I am an old man and have known a great many troubles, but most of them never happened."

8

Thinking Aloud: Talk

o o o o o o o o o o o o o o o o o o o o o o o o o o o o o o

Calvin Coolidge, the 30th president of the U.S., had a reputation for being reticent. One evening, a lady sitting next to him at dinner tried to coax him into talking to her.

"I have made a bet, Mr. Coolidge, that I could get more than two words out of you."

"You lose," replied Coolidge.

What style Coolidge had—he simply would not be made to talk. You have that choice too. Up until this chapter we've investigated ways for you to intervene with your Rat Brain internally. You can probably shift a problem situation without saying a word. That's some powerful magic—you can change your reality by conducting secret experiments. All you need now is a cape and a sidekick.

Sometimes though, talking can be the best course of action. A quick caveat—the way you have approached this type of conversation in the past was probably less than ideal; Rat Brain likes to fault others, to assert the winning opinion, and to look good. In police dramas the good cop/bad cop routine is used to break someone down—Rat Brain is like that but without the good cop. So, when you've talked about delicate issues before it may not have gone well for good reason. Remember the "active listening" skill of paraphrasing? Where you say back what you've heard the talker say? I knew that one but, in the not too distant past, I wouldn't do it. Because, to me, if I even voiced the other person's perspective, that meant they had won. That was simply not going to happen. Predictably, when we're coming from our mighty Rat Brain, conversations become painful.

But in actuality, talking to someone who matters to you about your Rat Brain is an honorable, even loving, thing to do. Here's why. They're having an impact on you they may not have a clue about—it's not fair to expect them to change if you haven't communicated with them. Talking about the issue gives them a chance—a chance for understanding, a chance to be closer, a chance to learn about their impact on you. You're also letting them know you better—what makes you crazy, what lights you up, how your thinking works. It doesn't have to be all kisses and hugs, but at the very least, learning will happen.

I call these conversations "Leaving the Rat Brain Loop" (or "Leaving the Loop" for short). The first memorable one I bumbled through was with my boss of the so-called out-of-control temper, Peter. After a couple of weeks of acting like a twit, I decided to talk to him about the staff meeting that had started it all. One morning, I dared myself to go to his office on the 5th floor. Once there, I managed to ask him if this was a good time for a chat. He smiled, pushed his chair away from his computer, and said, "Sure—have a seat."

"I'll come back later. This is a bad time."

"No, no. The whole day is open."

"You don't need to finish what you're working on?"

"What's on your mind?"

I mumbled. "Remember the staff meeting a couple of weeks ago?

"What?"

"The staff meeting!"

He nodded gently.

I took a breath. "Well, I have a question for you. You left the meeting early and I've been wondering about it." There I'd done it.

"I left the meeting?"

Good Lord, I thought. It was such a non-big deal for him that he doesn't remember. But I had to find out.

"We were talking about an assistant for Lindsay. And just after noon, when we were supposed to stop...

"Right, I do remember. I had a conference call."

"A phone call?"

"I needed to give someone a reference. I had already canceled a couple of times. I didn't want to make the person I was recommending look bad. I snuck out so I wouldn't interrupt you guys."

"A group of five people wouldn't notice you leaving?"

He laughed. "I hadn't thought about that."

"You are the big boss, you know. I thought you'd lost your temper with us." I clasped my hands together to keep from wagging my finger at him.

"Why would you think that?"

"When we started the meeting you said, 'We can talk about this until noon.' And then, when we went past noon, you left."

"I wanted to be sure we went to lunch. This group likes to skip meals—I don't. And I had that call."

So I was completely wrong. I couldn't fathom it. How could I have misread him so completely? Suddenly, I heard myself asking, "Where'd you get that tattoo?"

"The tattoo—I try to keep it covered but it doesn't always work."

Braver I asked, "What is it—a spider?"

He pulled his sleeve up. We both gazed at the dark blue blur. It was a scorpion.

"You've had that for a while?"

"Since I was young and stupid—in the Navy."

"How long were you in?"

"Five years. A long time ago."

"My father is retired Air Force so that makes me a military brat."

He squinted at me. "That explains a lot."

I laughed, surprised.

There was a knock on his door. Peter's secretary needed his signature on a few forms. I gathered my things and stood to go.

"To be continued," I announced.

"Darn right!" he replied.

Out in the hallway, I giggled—he was kind of fun. I couldn't believe I had asked about his tattoo. But it was at the heart of my worries about his temper. At that time, tattoos were not widely worn—especially by head honchos. So, at a level I hadn't noticed, I had linked it to his anger. And the question popped out of my mouth. Afterward, I was glad—I hadn't known that Peter was a Navy man, that he had ever been young and stupid, or that he tried to hide his tattoo. He became human to me that day.

Do We Have To?

Our desire to be free, self-determining, and to boldly go wherever we want to is an exhilarating part of our design. Unfortunately, we also like to give advice, opinions, and directives that were not asked for. Consider how much of our lives we spend trying to make others do what we want them to. And also try to avoid doing what they want us to do. The irony is that bossing people around doesn't usually work. Every age group on the planet can relate to that childhood complaint, "You're not the boss of me."

William Glasser, the author of *Choice Theory,* believes that the world's woes stem entirely from issues of control. When we feel that we're trapped and have no choice, we focus on resisting that control. The same is true when we try to control other people—they become rebellious. In Glasser's approach, we still have our opinions but we don't use them as weapons of superiority or punishment. Instead, you hold yourself as worthy of the freedom you seek. And hold other people as worthy of the independence they desire. Thus, looking to yourself and your Rat Brain is the most powerful way to create change. You, individually, have the ability to free yourself. And to free others.

The people in our lives want us to get along, to have good relationships, to keep things easy. Talking about the issues that trouble us clears the way for these kinds of relationships. To earn deep relationships, we have to brave. Talking about misunderstandings and mistakes is a courageous thing to do—other people know and respect this. You're letting another person in on how you see things, how your mind works, and how willing you are to improve your relationship with them. Not by beating on your chest, or proving you're tough, but by showing your humanity, that you are interested in them knowing you, and you knowing them. There is power in the vulnerability of going first, of self-disclosing—it's the noble road. And it leads to connection and trust.

In the book, *Crucial Conversations,* the authors recommend that we plan for an important talk by "Starting with Heart." First, this means asking yourself, "What do I really want here?" When Rat Brain is activated and your adrenalin is pumping, your first reaction may be to defend yourself or to put someone in their place. But the outcome of that will not be useful. So when you have all of your wits about you, it's a good time to decide on your true goal. What's the change that you want? You could want your spouse to be more reliable, or your employees to cut costs, or your neighbor to stop parking in your front yard.

The second part of creating a clear goal is to include what you don't want. You may want your son to spend less money and you do not want to argue. You might want your colleague to stop smacking her gum and you don't want to offend her. What's unexpectedly important in this is using the conjunction "and" in your goal. Not "but"—"but" implies that you cannot have what you want without paying a price. However, it is entirely possible to have a meaningful, honest conversation that's also encouraging, safe, and supportive.

Once you've sorted out what you do and don't want for the conversation, you'll want to keep that goal front and center. At any moment during your chat, Rat Brain will try to tempt you away from your Start with Heart path. You may suddenly try to save face or defer to authority or turn a cold shoulder. So, to focus on the here and now with this person, keep your true goal close to you. Because the next critical step is to imagine, "How would I behave if I really wanted these results?"

The Talking Cure

The overall approach to a Leaving the Loop conversation is to describe your trip through Rat Brain. In the best interest of your mental health, here's an important tip: If you want to prove someone wrong, or have them see the light, or make them beg for forgiveness, using these steps will not help you. (If I knew how to get those results, I would certainly tell you about it.) Rather, you're going to admit that you don't have the whole picture, that you're willing to take a look with them, and that you're prepared to change your mind. And you're going to ask for their perspective too. See how different that feels?

When you want to Leave the Loop, an invitation is a good place to start. The idea is to set up the conversation to succeed. That means finding a time and place that suits both of you. And specifically an invitation means that they get to say yes, no, or make a counter-offer. You don't want someone to feel they're obliged to talk to you. If they want to know your topic, which is a fair question, please don't start with, "You're an unhinged psychotic." That may be your Rat Brain's summary but it won't take you very far. Offer them a contextual headline, "Yesterday, when we talked about the Easter Egg Hunt, I think I misunderstood something. Just want to clear it up."

The place to start your conversation is Part 1 of the Rat Brain Loop, the observable data about what happened. In the meeting yesterday (or at breakfast this morning or at the airport last week) we talked about this topic, you said this and then I said that. Here you want to own up to how you remember it—this is what stood out for you, even if it didn't for them. You can also check in with them and see what they remember. Leaving the Loop is not about the exactness of the data. The point is to resolve the feelings and impressions that were left behind. So it's okay if you remember events differently; your purpose is to talk through how you were affected by what you experienced.

That leads us to the next step where you then tell the story that you've made up. Basically, describe Part 2 of your Rat Brain Loop—the personal meaning you made about what happened. Right up front, though, be sure to say that your interpretation could be wrong. It's important to own that you're sharing *your* version of reality. This isn't a good time to accuse or blame the other person. Rather you're showing them the links between the meaning you made, the emotions you felt, and what you wondered about. So they can see how that worked. For instance, "When you said no to my cookies I was embarrassed. I thought you were afraid I was trying to poison you."

The final step is to ask them if that was the message they intended for you to receive. Simply ask, "Was that what you meant or was it something else?" You're giving them room to clarify what they were trying to communicate, what kind of impact they wanted to have on you. Often, in these conversations, people guffaw at my interpretation of what happened. This doesn't help my ego but it does speak to how off-target we usually are. And then they can explain a completely different point of view that I immediately understand and believe. The matter is cleared up that easily. Turns out my friend who refused the cookies was allergic to nuts. When I explained the cookies didn't have nuts she ate them—every one.

Learning, No Matter What

Occasionally my interpretation is accurate—so what do I do then? Rather than celebrate with an, "I knew it!" I need to stay interested in what the other person was trying to get across. Let's use my conversation with Peter as an example of the steps to use in that case. What if he had actually been mad? I would have asked him, "What angered you?" (So we could both see what triggers him.) What message did he want to send us by leaving the meeting? (So we could both see how effective it was.)

I would then explain the impact of his leaving on my own behavior—Part 4 of the Rat Brain Loop. How I had started worrying about what I said to him, based on my reaction to his abrupt departure. Was this what he wanted? If not, what would he rather have? For the future, I would ask him to tell me, early on, that he was losing his patience so we could immediately address it. And I would also ask permission to check in with him when I thought he was getting mad.

If your interpretation of their behavior was accurate, a Leaving the Loop talk gives the two of you a "do-over" opportunity. You get to choose what to create together from now on. You might ask your conversation partner to act in a different way next time. And they might ask you to act in a different way. If you're up for it, you can look at how you are impacting them, what they see as your contribution to the issue between the two of you, and what requests they might have of you. Gets your heart pumping doesn't it?

What if Peter said that he wasn't angry in the staff meeting but I didn't believe him? Interacting with someone you think is a liar can be quite a strain. The initial steps in the process are the same—I would still describe my Rat Brain Loop, how I read the situation, and how I reacted. I would check in with him on his version of what happened and ensure that he felt heard.

Then I would request that he help me work on my interpretation—that we clear this up together. For example, I might suggest that each Friday I would review the week to see if I thought he had been angry. If so, could I call him and talk? At the end of two months, we could review the results of the experiment. You can design any kind of checking-in process that'll work for the two of you. The point is for you both to learn more about how the other engages with the world.

To have this approach work, at least 10% of you needs to be willing to have your mind changed. 90% of you can remain unconvinced. But that 10% allows space for wondrous possibilities. So prop your mind open a little to honor your end of the bargain. Thankfully, though, you aren't the only one doing the work now. Because Peter knows I'm paying attention. I'm not overtly asking him to change nor am I forcing my opinion on him. But he is on notice. And as we gather experiences about his anger (or lack of it), we'll build an understanding of either my oversensitivity or his temper or both.

The meta-view of what's going on in these Leaving the Loop conversations is that you are teaching another person how to be effective with you and you are learning to be more effective with them. You're designing how to interact together in ways that will minimize miscommunications. I realize these chats might sound like they're too hard, or too gooey, or too much. That's Rat Brain whispering in your ear. Most Leaving the Loop conversations are less than 15 minutes long. We are so often wrong in our interpretations that it's usually clear, immediately, how ridiculous it all is. Every once in a while you'll need several conversations over an extended period of time to sort something out. Especially thorny issues may need tending and maintenance.

One valuable tool to use here is the "Clean Up Agreement." The two of you will undoubtedly make messes with each other in the future. Decide now on how to clean them up. Karen Kimsey-House, a co-founder of The Coaches Training Institute, showed me how this is done. She was training a group of new instructors (including me) who were nervous and trying too hard to please. Karen said, "If you ever need to tell me something that you're afraid to say—I promise you that I will not run away. I may go to the mat with you and get loud and red in the face but I will not leave or cut you out or not like you anymore. Deal?" We all breathed in relief. To this day, I feel completely safe with her.

Your version of a Clean Up Agreement can include whatever elements are important to you: If either one of us gets mad (or fails to follow through or doesn't show up), we let the other one know. How can we do that most effectively? What's the best way to connect? And what do we want as a result? Do we get in touch immediately or have a cooling off period? Do we like apologies or not? Do we stay with the conversation until it's done or do we take breaks? Who else can we talk to about this? Where's the best place to talk—the office, over lunch, on the phone, with a margarita? By talking about how to connect in the future, we're both now prepared to live through the next misunderstanding with less emotional angst. We have created a clear way out that wasn't there before.

Please don't be scared off. Try one Leaving the Loop talk once a week and see what shows up. What's the worst that could happen? (I promise you it won't happen.) Go easy on yourself and start with simpler conversations first. Think of yourself as a cultural anthropologist or an interpersonal detective. Celebrate every bit of progress, both forward and backward, in your experiments—because learning what works, and what does not, is what matters. As the writer Marcel Proust said, "The real voyage of discovery consists not in seeking new landscapes, but in having new eyes."

Leaving the Loop

Here are the steps for Leaving the Loop. After each step, there's an example of what could be said. While it's important to include all of the steps in a Leaving the Loop talk, you can say them in any way that works. And while I don't point it out in the steps specifically, humor, lightness, or self-deprecation will only make things easier. Bon Voyage.

Step 1—Invitation:

Example: "I have something on my mind and I'd like to talk with you about it. Could we chat for about 15 minutes? When's a good time?"

Your Version:

_____

_____

Step 2—Inaccuracy:

Example: "I may be out in left field here so I want to check in with you—" or "I've made up a story which is confusing to me so I'd like to talk it through with you—"

Your Version:

_____

_____

Step 3—Willingness To Change:

Example: "I want to be sure that I understand what you want—I'm willing to look at how I may be responsible for why this isn't working—" or "I like to be right, as you know, but I want to put that aside for now. Will you look at this with me and see where we need to tweak it—"

Your Version:

_____

_____

Step 4—What Happened:

Describe Part 1 (Selected Info.) of your Rat Brain Loop.

Example: "What I remember is that you said that I didn't know the words to the National Anthem. Then, I stuck my tongue out at you—"

Your Version:

_____

_____

Step 5—Meaning Made:

Describe Part 2 (Define Meaning) of your Rat Brain Loop.

Example: "I thought you meant I wasn't a good citizen and that made me mad. Sticking out my tongue was my way of telling that I do too know the words."

Your Version:

_____

_____

Step 6—Intended Message:

Example: "What message did you want me to receive—" or "What were you hoping I would do or not do when you did that—"

Your Version:

_____

_____

These steps are a good guideline for a Leaving the Loop discussion. You might use every one of them or just a few. In some places you may need more detail but in others very little. Among the most important things to have with you, though, are your heartfelt goal and a willingness to own your part in the problem. This approach provides a middle way for self-expression. You don't have to settle for either keeping quiet or attacking like a cobra. This is a time to say what's important to you with courage and power.

The Leverage of Talk

One of my clients, a Director at "McTech," had a group of highly technical design engineers who were missing deadlines and kept asking to be re-assigned. They were a talented bunch, working on an elite project. What was going on? I spent some time with the group to put together the big picture.

There were a couple of important dynamics at work in this department. One was that Daniel, the senior leader, was often missing in action. Deeply introverted, Daniel was better at thinking than interacting with people. With such invisible leadership at the top, two other managers were offering direction to the group. But Tony and Ken didn't want to anger or embarrass Daniel so they were managing behind his back.

Tony was a powerfully built fireplug of a man. He talked fast, thought fast, moved fast. Feeling that he was carrying the weight of the project on his back, Tony disdained Ken's "slow and steady" attitude. Ken was a tall, slender man with pale eyes sheltered by thick glasses. He had a calming influence on the people around him. He struggled with shepherding the group while reining in Tony.

Naturally, Ken and Tony had different ideas about how to move forward with their project. Soon, everyone knew that they disagreed on several points of engineering. But because Ken and Tony were managing around Daniel, everything felt clandestine. People in the group started to rally, secretly of course, around the manager they liked better. Once they chose a side, the covert joys of gossiping, complaining, and withholding information became theirs. Productivity plummeted.

It was time to dust for Rat Brain's fingerprints; Ken, Tony, and I examined their habits. Ken admitted that, in meetings, he felt that Tony was stirring up opposition against him. But Ken was determined to remain calm—he didn't want to be goaded into public disagreements—so he withdrew. Tony, for his part, was trying to turn around the mood of the group—this meant waking up the troops, offering provocative viewpoints, being all-around noisy. Particularly, he pointed out, because Ken rarely said anything in meetings.

Alas, the buffer Ken was trying to create between he and Tony had the opposite effect he was hoping for; it actually made Tony louder and more insistent. And Tony in trying to encourage people to engage with him was shutting them down. When we talked through this they both groaned with recognition. I told them they reminded me of a cartoon: A man and a woman are in a tiny sailboat. There is no wind, not a single wave—it's a perfectly calm day. But the woman is leaning far out over the starboard side of the boat trying to keep the boat upright. Because the man is leaning far out over the portside of the boat—in order to balance against her. If they both would stop working so hard and come back inside the boat, they might enjoy the day.

Within an hour Tony and Ken had decided on how to break their cycle. No more acting like they weren't trying to lead—they were leading. The two of them would meet once a week to hash out either a united front or their list of different opinions. Any decisions they couldn't make, they would take to the Director. They would both present in the engineering meetings—with equal time for each of them to speak. They also discussed how to stop this pattern from developing again and designed some partnering agreements. Once, they even smiled at each other.

I visited with the group a couple of weeks later. Everything was calmer, no real issues now. Would I come to their potluck luncheon? To see if I was dreaming, I pinched one of them. What had happened to all the intrigue? Amazingly, a few days after Ken and Tony had re-connected, the cliques had dissolved. Three months later, to everyone's surprise, that endangered program produced an amazing product, on time, and within budget.

The Joy Of Thinking

The automatic aspects of our brains are interested in efficiency, in having things make sense, in fitting current events into what we already know. We are designed to classify, categorize and rationalize. Usually, we continue to look for evidence that confirms what we already know. The neural pathways—the physical places that make connections and meanings in our brains—that we use most frequently become stronger and more prominent. In fact, neurological science is discovering that we actually develop ruts in our brains.

Just like a path in the woods, the more the path is used, the more likely it will be used again. And what a convenience paths are—the brush has been cleared away, nettles won't poke or sting you, and most obstacles have been removed. You can see where you're going and arrive there quickly. It takes far less energy to use a path that's already in place. And when a neural pathway becomes so well-used that it's upgraded from dirt road to pavement, you can speed along it in your TUV (Thought Utility Vehicle).

What can be compelling about these ruts, in a terrible way, is how easy it is to stay in them. If the fastest, simplest thing to do is feel insulted or angry or ignored, why wouldn't you? These ruts can become as concrete to us—as real—as a highway superstructure. But these roads won't lead us to where we truly want to go.

Fortunately, we have much more available to us than our Rat Brains. And the fun of having a Big Brain is in using it. We have an amazing facility for rational detachment that let's us observe how our Rat Brain works. We also have enormous capacities for kindness and generosity. These are the tools we need to squelch Rat Brain. Compassion, a general kind of love, allows us to sympathize with the people in our lives. The key is to focus on our connection, our common humanity. Then it becomes clear that every one of us deserves respect, help, and care. Mother Teresa said, "If you judge people, you don't have time to love them." When our minds fill up with automatic judgments, generosity is crowded out. But with a Big Brain, you can choose a different path.

Each of us is faced with choices to make about what to do, how to act, who to be. This, then, is life lived to the fullest—making decisions, taking action, and being responsible for all of it. It's true that we are simply handed many aspects of our existence; the critical point, though, is what we do with what we've been given. What our existence amounts to is ours to determine. Given our place and time, we can make something of ourselves. We can choose who we become. Our calling is to live lives that are filled with passion, self-understanding, and commitment. Your mission, if you choose to accept it, is deep engagement with the world.

Bibliography

Diane Ackerman, *A Natural History of the Senses*. New York: Random House, 1990.

Arbinger Institute (editors), *Leadership and Self Deception: Getting Out of the Box*. San Francisco: Berrett-Koehler Publishers, 2002

Chris Argyris, *Overcoming Organizational Defenses: Facilitating Organizational Learning*. Needham Heights, MA: Allyn and Bacon, 1990.

Aaron Ben-Ze'ev, *The Subtlety of Emotions*. Cambridge, Massachusetts: The MIT Press, 2000.

Andre Bernard and Clifton Fadiman, *Bartlett's Book of Anecdotes*. New York: Little, Brown, and Company, 2006.

David Bohm, *On Dialogue*. Ojai, CA: David Bohm Seminars, 1990.

Marion Zimmer Bradley, *The Mists of Avalon*. New York: Ballantine, 1982.

Richard E. Cytowic, *The Man Who Tasted Shapes*. New York: G.P. Putnam's Sons, 1993.

Antonio Damasio, *The Feeling of What Happens: Body and Emotion In The Making Of Consciousness*. Orlando: Harcourt, 1999.

Antonio Damasio, *Descartes' Error: Emotion, Reason, and the Human Brain*. New York: Penguin Putnam, 1994.

Susan Engel, *Context Is Everything: The Nature of Memory*. New York: W.H. Freeman and Company, 1999.

Victor Frankl, *Man's Search For Meaning*. Boston: Beacon Press, 1959, 1962, 1985.

Malcolm Gladwell, *Blink: The Power of Thinking Without Thinking*. Brown, Little, and Company, 2005.

William Glasser, *Choice Theory: A New Psychology of Personal Freedom*. New York: HarperCollins, 1998.

Daniel Goleman, *Emotional Intelligence: Why It Can Matter More Than IQ*. New York: Bantam Books, 1995.

Jeff Jacobson, *Hard Left: One Man's Life on Four Wheels*. Dir. Christine McHugh. DVD. San Francisco, 2006.

Victor S. Johnson, *Why We Feel: The Science of Human Emotions*. New York: Perseus Books, 1999.

Joseph LeDoux, *The Emotional Brain: The Mysterious Underpinnings of Emotional Life*. New York: Simon & Schuster, 1996.

Thomas Lewis and Fari Amini and Richard Lannon, *A General Theory of Love*. New York: Vintage Books, 2001.

Jennifer L. Leo (editor), *Sand In My Bra: Funny Women Write From The Road*. San Francisco: Travelers' Tales, 2003.

Elizabeth Loftus and Katherine Ketchum, *The Myth of Repressed Memory: False Memories & Allegations of Sexual Abuse*. New York: St. Martin's Press, 1994.

Elizabeth Loftus and Katherine Ketchum, *Witness for the Defense: The Accused, The Eyewitness, and the Expert Who Puts Memory on Trial*. New York: St. Martin's Press, 1991.

Paul MacLean, *The Triune Brain in Evolution: Role in Paleocerebral Functions*. New York: Springer, 1990.

Bill O'Hanlon, *Do One Thing Different: And Other Uncommonly Sensible Solutions to Life's Persistent Problems*. New York: HarperCollins, 1999.

Kerry Patterson and Joseph Grenny and Ron McMillan and Al Switzler, *Crucial Conversations: Tools for Talking When Stakes are High*. New York: McGraw-Hill, 2002.

Rashomon, Dir. Akira Kurosawa, DVD, Criterion Collection, 1950.

Robert Rosenthal and Lenore Jacobson, *Pygmalion in the Classroom*. New York: Holt, Rinehart & Winston, 1968.

Daniel L. Schacter, *The Seven Sins of Memory: How The Mind Forgets And Remembers*. New York: Houghton Mifflin, 2001.

Peter Senge, *The Fifth Discipline: The Art And Practice of the Learning Organization*. New York: Doubleday, 1990.

Peter Senge and Art Kleiner and Charlotte Roberts and Rick Ross and Bryan Smith, *The Fifth Discipline Fieldbook*. New York: Doubleday, 1994.

Douglas Stone and Bruce Patton and Sheila Heen, *Difficult Conversations: How To Discuss What Matters Most*. New York: Viking, 1999.

Anne Ursu, *Spilling Clarence: A Novel*. New York: Hyperion, 2002.

Diane Vaughan, *The Challenger Launch Decision: Risky Technology, Culture, and Deviance at NASA*. Chicago: University of Chicago Press, 1996.

Paul Watzlawick and John Weakland and Richard Fisch, *Change: Principles of Problem Formation and Problem Resolution*. New York: W.W. Norton, 1974.

Bill Watterson, *The Indispensable Calvin & Hobbes*. Kansas City: Andrews and McMeel, 1992.

Michelle Weiner-Davis, *Fire Your Shrink! Do-It-Yourself Strategies For Changing Your Life and Everyone In It*. New York: Simon & Schuster, 1995.

Laura Whitworth and Henry Kimsey-House and Phil Sandhal, *Co-Active Coaching: New Skills for Coaching People Toward Success In Work and Life*. Mountain View, CA: Davies-Black Publishing, 1998.

Robert Wright, *The Moral Animal: Evolution in Psychology and Everyday Life*. New York: Vintage Books, 1995.

Irvin Yalom, *Love's Executioner & Other Tales of Psychotherapy*. New York: Harper Perennial, 1989.

Cindy Yarbrough, *Thrown For a Loss: My Brother's Journey From Fame Into Madness*. Prepublication Copy, 2005.

Call for Stories!

I'd be delighted to hear your Rat Brain Loop stories. Whether your experience was a silly misunderstanding, an upsetting argument, or a surprising interpretation, please tell me about it. You might have misunderstood the data or you wildly misjudged the situation. Or perhaps someone else misinterpreted or misunderstood you.

Whatever happened, I'd love to hear it. Rat Brain stories have so much to teach us about our automatic thinking. What have you learned?

Please send your stories to me at my email address: Lauren@LaurenPowers.net

Index

978-0-595-39396-1
0-595-39396-9

Printed in the United States
110133LV00004B/154-165/A